Praise for Mary & Me

"*Mary & Me* is a powerful testament to the beauty of friendship as told through decades of letter writing. In a disarmingly personal depiction, Kenyon and Humston lead us through a story of friendship that withstands time, distance, and all the joy and heartache that life can offer."

—HEATHER GUDENKAUF
New York Times and *USA Today* bestselling author

"This book is a pure tribute to friendship, letter writing, and, most of all, love. The shared experiences of loss, faith, and letting go between Mary and Mary aren't just inspiring—they're enough to push you out of your own comfort zone to be a little braver today. No doubt, this is the sort of story that will make you want to try harder, love people better, hold the good ones in your life tighter, and leave no collection of words left unsaid. In short, this book captures the real stuff of life. The real stuff."

—HANNAH BRENCHER
Creator of MoreLoveLetters.com,
TED speaker, and author of *If You Find This Letter*

"Through friendship and a treasure trove of handwritten letters, *Mary & Me* shows how our connections to one another make life precious. Mary Potter Kenyon and Mary Jedlicka Humston have given us the gift of a heartfelt and endearing memoir that will stand the test of time."

—JOHN SCHLIMM
Award-winning author of *Five Years in Heaven:
The Unlikely Friendship That Answered Life's Greatest Questions*

"A book about the joy of letters is always a cause of celebration, and when it is also a book about the incomparable consolations of friendship expressed through letters, the celebration is even greater. *Mary & Me* offers beautiful proof that there is no better demonstration of true friendship than through letters: shared confidences that address our sorrows, our joys, and our need for each other."

—NINA SANKOVITCH
Bestselling author of *Tolstoy and the Purple Chair* and
Signed, Sealed, Delivered: Celebrating the Joys of Letter Writing

"Mary Kenyon is one of those rare women who walked into my world and became an instant lifelong friend. She exudes love of family, faith, integrity, and beauty, and those things shine in her writing and relationships. *Mary & Me: A Lasting Link Through Ink*, cowritten with Mary Jedlicka Humston, offers rich wisdom about the art of friendship and the beauty of commitment that goes beyond the limits of time and space. Mary and Mary show how words enrich us, give us life, and bond our spirits and souls."

—SHELLY BEACH
Christy Award–winning author of twelve books and
coauthor of *Love Letters from the Edge*

"The letter writing that conspired weekly for nearly thirty years to create this book is a model of friendship and love that makes me wish to turn back the clock and re-create this for my own life. The world would be a more beautiful place if everyone would engage with each other in the same way that the Marys have."

—WENDY WOLFF
Author of *The Letter Writing Project*

"In this book, the two Marys focus on friendship through the written word, two topics near and dear to my heart. For twenty-five years, I have made my living as a writer, and although I love my job, it is when I put my pen to paper and write to my friends that I feel happiest. Sharing my life and inner thoughts with someone who listens, cares, and responds, even if that friend is miles away, is key to my well-being. This book is a wonderful reminder of how much we need others, and how, for many of us, that comfort, joy, and happiness comes in an envelope in the mailbox."

—TAMARA ORR

Author of *A Parent's Guide to Homeschooling*

and over 400 children's books

Mary & Me

Linda—
To my new tea-time
friend! ☺
Always treasure your friends

♡ Mary Jedlicka Humston

Published by Familius LLC, www.familius.com

Familius books are available at special discounts for bulk purchases for sales promotions
or for family or corporate use. Special editions, including personalized covers, excerpts of
existing books, or books with corporate logos, can be created in large quantities for special
needs. For more information, contact Premium Sales at 559-876-2170 or email
specialmarkets@familius.com.

Library of Congress Catalog-in-Publication Data
2015942864

Print ISBN 9781942934028
Ebook ISBN 9781942934325
Hardcover ISBN 9781942934332

Printed in the United States of America

Edited by Hannah Chudleigh
Cover design by David Miles
Book design by Brooke Jorden
Illustrations by Freepik, Fotolia, and Silhouette Studio

10 9 8 7 6 5 4 3 2 1

First Edition

Mary & Me

A LASTING LINK THROUGH INK

MARY POTTER KENYON &
MARY JEDLICKA HUMSTON

Acknowledgments

Mary Potter Kenyon

Behind every author, there is a team of players that makes writing a book possible. For each of my books, there have been two key encouragers who no longer reside on this earth: my mother, Irma Rose Potter, and the husband who shared my life for thirty-four years, David Edward Kenyon. This particular book is also made possible because of the support of my eight children, particularly the three that lived with me during the months I completed it: Emily Rose, Katherine Terese, and Abigail Grace. I hope that by seeing their mother follow her dreams, they will never hesitate to follow their own.

If it seems strange to also thank one's cowriter in an acknowledgement, well then, I am guilty of being an oddity, because this book wouldn't exist without Mary. Everyone should have their own Mary.

I would be remiss if I didn't thank my brother, Lyle Potter, and his wife Cindy, for their generous offer of a writing retreat in their beautiful home in Cedar Falls.

And, of course, I express my gratitude to the many new friends I have made just in the last five years, some whose essays grace these pages, and those whose hearts have touched my own. Special thanks to Shelly Beach, who has been bravely battling health issues, and whose grace and spirit of friendship has blessed me and countless others.

Mary Jedlicka Humston

Thanks to my husband Jim, whose love and support for me and my writing has never wavered.

Thanks also to Jill and Andrew (Asher and Orrin), Liz and Greg (Zoey), and Jon and Tina (Levi), who've given me love, love, love.

Many thanks to my parents, who always believed in me, and to Jim's and my siblings and their spouses, who have been through thick and thin with me.

Thanks to all my dear, dear friends from high school, college, teaching, playgroup, church, TOPS, PEO, Christian Women's Club, and Bible studies; neighbors; and those from so many other walks of my life: your friendship and encouragement bless me beyond measure.

Thanks to the University Club Writers of Iowa City and the Iowa City Branch of the National League of American Pen Women (and past groups: John Tigges' Dubuque writing group and The Cottage Writers), who have all helped me become a much better writer.

And, lastly, my love and thanks to my dear friend Mary Potter Kenyon. I am privileged to have cowritten *Mary & Me: A Lasting Link Through Ink* with you. I will always treasure the journey we have taken. Now, wait. Hold on. I need to go write you a letter about all this before I forget the details.

The Marys thank all our guest essayists for the wonderful way their unique stories of friendship enriched *Mary & Me*. We would also like to thank Jill Humston, winner of our subtitle contest, and Daniel Kenyon, photographer for our back cover author photo.

Contents

Foreword

The act of writing letters grants us the ability to mull over what we want to discuss or how we want to respond. This consideration is a luxury not granted to us in typical conversation. These quiet moments for letters, carved out of spare time throughout the day, have been extremely important to Mary Kenyon and Mary Humston since the beginning of their correspondence. Despite interruptions to their writing due to the chaos of life, letters allowed their connection to be placed on pause until they were able to pick back up where they left off. The ability to read or write a letter on their own time, savoring it over tea or as a nightcap before bed, built the base to their friendship. These letters are a gift of the writer's time.

As the founders of the Letter Writers Alliance, we are not immune to those same interruptions that Mary and Mary faced. When Kathy was on a deadline for a graphic design proposal and just needed to find that one thing to complete the project, she flipped through an art book in search of inspiration, and a letter fell from the pages onto her lap. The letter was from Donovan and had been delivered years ago to reassure Kathy of her ability to complete a graduate thesis that would knock her advisor's socks off. In opening and reading the letter years later, this calming moment was revisited. As Kathy sat on the office floor, Donovan was reassuring her in both past and present.

The friendship between us had strengthened while that letter lay dormant in that random book, but the letter lost none of its power.

When we started the Letter Writers Alliance in 2007, we assumed it would be something for our own amusement. It would consist of our small circle of friends who still wrote letters on occasion. We were con-vinced that our enthusiasm for letters was a rarified one, and that the L.W.A. would be a quirky little group that would fit into one address book. We are still amazed that, at the time this is published, we have over eight thousand members.

In running the L.W.A., we have discovered that one theme contin-ues to bring people to letter writing: connection. As Mary Humston and Mary Kenyon connect through their letter writing, their correspondence joins their lives in a common space—each person learning from the other a different way to experience our world. Letters connect people of all dif-ferent backgrounds and place them on equal footing. We are pen pals with people we would have never met in our daily lives. Even though Mary and Mary met as neighbors, their bond would not have been possi-ble through normal social events.

As the Kenyon family moved to different homes, Mary and Mary could virtually summon each other to their side through their letters. While they wrote in their own environment, they felt linked to each other over all the miles apart. As it is with all letters, your friend is there with you as you write to them or as you read a response from them. Letters contain an almost confessional quality, making you feel like you are having an intimate conversation with the correspondent at that very moment. Thoughts that you had no idea were on your mind find their way in a letter through the cathartic act of writing. This is the choice Mary and Mary made in their relationship: to stay connected in both tangible and intangible ways.

For thirty years, the Marys have maintained their correspondence, their connection empowered by sheets of paper. Through their let-ters, these two friends have been able to get through extremely difficult moments and grow as mothers, friends, and community members. Their commitment to each other is apparent within these pages. One cannot help but smile when reading how Mary Kenyon and Mary Humston have flourished through their friendship. Career uncertainty, doubts in child rearing, constant relocation, and even cancer could not hamper the support and love these two have for each other. The story of Mary and Mary's friendship speaks volumes of the strengths we can find in relationships nurtured through letters.

Letters are more than a communication of events; they are a tangible representation of affection. A whole range of emotions are felt before one even opens the envelope. It isn't even about the contents of the letter. It's that someone sent a letter at all. Such a simple thing to cause such complex feelings. What a gift to give and to receive. The simple gift these Marys have shared over the years are now shared with you. With this book, the Kenyon and Humston children have a historical paper trail of their mothers' lives and the building of their friendship—a priceless legacy of bundled correspondence that will breathe life into their memories. Moments sprinkled down the path of life, bound within the pages you hold before you. Enjoy the unfurling of these memories, one by one, as we have.

Sincerely,

Ms. Kathy Zadrozny & Mrs. Donovan Beeson Yothers
Founders of the Letter Writers Alliance

Introduction

I have long felt that if a writer cannot write a letter that will move someone, writing a book that moves a lot of someones may be too much to expect of her.

—Robert Benson, *Dancing on the Head of a Pen*

The length of the friendship never brought astonishment. After all, the majority of Baby Boomers could likely claim a long-standing friendship in their lives. No, it was always the letters: the-pen-on-paper, inside-a-stamped-envelope, mailed-in-a-mailbox letter that was awe inspiring.

"You've been writing a letter every week for almost thirty years?" The question always evokes disbelief, particularly since the dawn of the Internet and email. We quickly correct the misconception.

"Well, at least one letter, but usually more. We write each other three or four letters a week. And we never wait for a return letter before beginning another."

Conservatively speaking, at just three letters a week since 1987, that would equal 4,368 letters each, but we'd both agree that estimate is much too low. We have, on occasion, written each other two letters in a single day.

Not long ago, I was the featured speaker for one of the many groups Mary is a member of. The subject was writing and my success at having three books published. At the conclusion of the presentation, I welcomed questions from the audience. My answer to "How did you two Marys meet?" included mention of our letter-writing relationship. Astonished gasps echoed from each corner of the room.

"What do you plan on writing next?" another woman asked.

I looked across the room at Mary. She knew of my struggle to write since I'd completed a two-year book project detailing the loss of my mother, husband, and grandson in the space of three years.

Our eyes met, and a jolt of electricity shot through me. Mary would comment later that she'd felt it too, and she knew what I was going to say before I even said it.

"I think . . . " I faltered, my eyes still locked with hers.

"I think I'm supposed to write a book with Mary, a book about our friendship," I blurted out, then added with a laugh, "and I didn't know that until I just said it out loud."

This book explores a friendship that began in June 1986 and will most likely not end until "death do us part." The fact that one of the women in this relationship had never really had other female friends outside of her sisters, while the other woman had too many to count, is all part of the story.

For many years, ours was primarily a letter-writing friendship with a few face-to-face visits now and then. That changed in November 2011 when we traveled six hours together to attend a writer's conference and stayed at a motel for a few nights, giving us plenty of opportunity to discuss subjects we hadn't broached before, effectively deepening our relationship.

Numerous studies show that recovery from a major health challenge, such as a heart attack or cancer, is enhanced because of friendship. The continuing Nurses' Health Study from Harvard Medical School has found that the more friends a woman has, the less likely she is to develop physical impairments as she ages, and the more likely she is to be lead-ing a joyful life.[1] When researchers looked at how well the women func-tioned after the death of their spouse, they found that even in the face of this biggest stressor of all, those women who had a close friend and

1. www.channing.harvard.edu/nhs

confidante were more likely to survive the experience without any new physical impairments or permanent loss of vitality. I learned the truth of that study in March 2012, just a few months after Mary and I had shared that overnight trip.

In fact, on the morning of March 27, 2012, I'd been sitting on the couch writing a letter to Mary when I decided to wake my husband for his coffee. For at least thirty minutes, I'd been sitting within arm's reach of David's chair, where he sat with his eyes closed. When I leaned over, touching his arm and whispering his name, he did not respond.

I didn't even know he was gone, I would repeat over and over to my sisters. *How could I not know? I was just sitting there, drinking coffee and writing a letter to Mary, and all the while my husband was dead.*

"I have it. I brought it with me," Mary broached the subject during one of our writing sessions.

"Have what?"

"The letter you were writing that morning. I saved it in case you wanted it."

I hesitated briefly. "I want it."

It was several days before I opened it. As I read the beginning of the letter dated March 27, 2012, I imagined sitting on the couch with a cup of coffee, David in the chair nearby. Suddenly, *I was there*, on that fateful March morning. My written words reminded me why I was going to wake David up. It wasn't for a cup of coffee, as I'd imagined for more than two years, though I'm sure I would have offered to get him a cup. No, instead I'd just shared something in my letter to Mary that I hadn't yet told David. I'd just related an incident that had occurred the night before: when I'd walked up to the podium to speak at a workshop, people in the audience stood up and clapped. It had been so fantastical, so unbelievable. Clapping—for me! I'd been so tired when I'd arrived home that I'd forgotten to mention it. The reason I was going to wake David was to tell him. I knew he'd get a kick out of it. His support was behind everything

I did then—the writing, workshops, and public speaking. He reveled in all my recent successes, successes I'd often assured him I wouldn't have without him.

I wanted David to be the first to hear about the clapping. I couldn't wait to tell him. I never got that chance.

Did the letter lay abandoned on the couch after I discovered he was gone? Was it there while the paramedics worked futilely over his body? I don't remember. At some point it ended up on my desk, where I picked it up again on April 2, a week later. This was a pivotal point in our letter-writing relationship. Initially, I felt ill at the thought of writing Mary because that was what I was doing right before discovering my husband was dead. Would something as ugly and horrifying as my husband's unexpected death mar our long-standing relationship? I confessed my worry to Mary in that first letter after. She had wondered the same thing. Thankfully, once I got past the hurdle of the initial correspondence, I never felt that discomfort again, and our avid letter-writing relationship resumed.

For the purpose of avoiding confusion, my essay will appear first with each topic, followed by my friend Mary Jedlicka Humston's essay. We have also included guest essays placed between chapters, displaying unique aspects of friendship from a small sampling of women through-out the country. The final section includes chapter-by-chapter discussion questions for groups and book clubs.

Mary Potter Kenyon

CHAPTER ONE

First Meetings

Dear Mary, do you remember
the day you two met?

Mary Potter Kenyon

I cannot count the number of mornings in the past twenty-eight years I started with a written narrative to Mary Humston. Long before Facebook existed, these "status reports" came in the form of handwritten letters. If they had been saved, they'd likely fill more than one massive trunk by now, because they were both frequent (sometimes as many as five or six in a week) and occasionally quite lengthy. Had we kept our mutual letters, they would have revealed far more about us than any journal could. Some days I wish I had them, for an intimate peek at my former self, the mother of three, then four, five, and ultimately eight children. Other days I am glad for their absence, not necessarily wanting to revisit the mind-boggling mess of minutiae that mothering a large brood included. There were many days, many *years*, when I struggled just to maintain a semblance of selfhood. Those letters to and from Mary were a sort of lifeline that kept me sane.

I was twenty-seven years old and pregnant with my third child when I met Mary in the summer of 1986. My husband David and I had just moved to Iowa City, where he would be taking master's courses in social work at the University of Iowa. New to the neighborhood in a large college town, I spent those first few days alternately unpacking boxes and sitting in a rocking chair near the window, wondering just what we were thinking. Why were we leaving the place where we'd met, married, and begun raising a family? *And where are all the young mothers?* I'd wonder as I searched the sidewalk for a telltale stroller.

The fact that my husband had completed his BA at the University of Northern Iowa in Cedar Falls, Iowa, where they did not offer a master's program, had something to do with our decision, but my doubts about moving would be well founded. Within a year, David decided he didn't want to pursue a master's after all, and we would return to Cedar Falls, where I began graduate courses in family services. Eighteen credits later, I abandoned that idea, realizing I needed to serve my rapidly expanding family's interest by becoming a stay-at-home mother. I attended my last college classes while pregnant with my fourth baby, taking finals from a hospital bed shortly after giving birth.

Of course, I couldn't have known any of that as I gazed out the window of the small rented house on Franklin Street during those first few days after our move. Within a week, and before I'd completely unpacked, there was a knock on the door. On my doorstep stood a dark-haired, friendly-faced woman with three young children in tow and a plate of homemade cookies in one hand.

"Welcome to the neighborhood," Mary chimed as she deftly thrust the cookies in my direction, simultaneously pulling the toddler, who clung desperately to the hem of her shirt, up into her arms. With that swift maneuver, her loose-fitting summer top bunched to the side, revealing a section of her bra. What Mary couldn't know was that it wasn't the neighborly gesture of cookies that won me over but that stray bra strap. I'd breastfed my first two children and planned on it for the third. I instantly recognized the telltale clip of a nursing bra.

For as long as I could remember, I'd yearned for a female friend, a kindred spirit, but I'd never known the secret to cultivating one. My elementary years were plagued with bullying, mostly from female instigators, and the friendships I managed to forge in high school seemed shallow after graduation, having stemmed mostly from convenience and shared extracurricular activities. I'd lost track of the majority of them within months of graduation. Until I met Mary, the only friends I'd maintained were my six sisters.

For those first seven years of my marriage, I'd been searching for the "perfect" friend, one who would understand and validate my attachment-parent mothering style, my Catholic beliefs that precluded any form of birth control, and the creative mind that itched to be writing. I'd yearned for someone just like me. Then I opened my door and there stood a woman who I learned was Catholic, into couponing and refunding just like me, loved to write, and was evidently a breastfeeding mom. Bingo! The clone I desired.

Only later would I discover that Mary was not my clone, but by then it was too late. A kinship had already developed between us. I credit her for that, since I had no idea how to form an adult female friendship. Had our relationship depended upon Mary meeting my strict requirements, it never would have continued. For one thing, it turned out Jonathan, their third child, was going to be their last, dispelling my prerequisite regarding birth control. As for the utilitarian nursing bra, Jonathan had abruptly weaned during an illness months before, and she hadn't gotten around to replacing it.

Mary's oldest daughter, Jill, was my son Dan's age and her Elizabeth the same age as my Elizabeth. For the next year, our proximity meant both Elizabeths would spend hours playing at each other's house and Dan would have a built-in friend to ease his way into a new school. It also meant that because of Mary, I would be introduced to the wonders of breastfeeding support in the form of a La Leche League group and the radical *Mothering* magazine that discussed such things as refusing vaccinations, vaginal births after a cesarean delivery, and the pros and cons of circumcision. Mary also invited me to what would be the first, and unfortunately the last, mother's playgroup I would live near. I attended it every Friday that year and was exposed to a cornucopia of women: straight-laced business-suit types, doctor's wives, women with children in private schools, those who combined careers with motherhood, homeschooling mothers, sling-wearing mamas who nursed two children simultaneously, and one woman whose bedroom consisted of a single gigantic mattress on the floor shared by the entire family. Mary might not have actually been living the lifestyle I was destined for, but she was definitely responsible for exposing me to a world that allowed for differences in mothering choices. While I never did form any other friendships during the year I lived in Iowa City, I got a glimpse into a world of female bonding, a world Mary seemed to take for granted and one through which she effortlessly navigated.

When my family returned to Cedar Falls, I resumed my college student/motherhood life. I left Iowa City with two new additions: a six-month-old baby and the ultimate pen pal, a copious letter writer named Mary.

We never discussed how we were going to maintain our relationship. We simply exchanged addresses upon our good-byes and promised to stay in touch. I would hazard a guess that a letter from Mary likely entered my mailbox within days of the move. A pattern emerged within weeks. Unlike other pen pal relationships I'd attempted to forge, Mary didn't even wait for me to answer one letter before beginning another. (This early pattern continues to this day, nearly thirty years later.) I began a letter to Mary first thing nearly every morning, sometimes concluding it by nightlight at the bedside of whichever child was the youngest at the time.

While we occasionally took time to address questions or comments in the other Mary's letters, we basically reported our daily lives to each other on paper. We were each other's journal. Telephone calls were not part of our relationship repertoire. Neither was email. With ninety miles between us, actual physical visits were few and far between. When they were arranged, it was amid the cacophony of a large group of children. Plus, I didn't have the time or energy for more socialization. It would be almost twenty years after that initial parting that Mary and I would spend time alone, sans children. So it was thousands of letters that maintained our friendship.

In the ensuing years after I left her neighborhood, I often proclaimed Mary as my "best friend," but she was actually my only friend, and from her letters, I was aware the same qualification didn't apply to me. I sometimes wondered at her claims: the breakfast out with two friends, then lunch with another, a Bible study with yet a different group of women, a standing movie night, teas, trips, and even a card-club night. *Really?* I would wonder skeptically. *Can anyone really have that many friends?* Because I didn't.

From the time I got married until a Christian writer's workshop in 2011, I could claim only a single female friend outside of my sisters : Mary. And for the majority of those years, I never knew what I was missing.

Mary Jedlicka Humston

When new neighbors moved up the street during the summer of 1986, I was delighted to note they were a family with children.

Meeting new people, especially mothers and their infants, toddlers, and preschoolers, was a common occurrence for me. So the fact that I don't remember the weather or what clothes my children and I wore when we met these neighbors doesn't rattle me. I don't recall how long we mothers talked or who said what. The time of day even escapes me, as does the day of the week. Did my children get antsy? Excited for new playmates? I'm embarrassed to admit I just can't remember. Perhaps she would stay only a short time and then leave, like so many others eventually did.

During my early parenting years in the '80s, living in a town with a Big Ten university frequently took a subtle, but significant, toll on me. So many couples my age (late twenties, early thirties) with young children came and went, staying for a few years until a University of Iowa degree or program was completed. Then they headed off, sometimes clear across the country, in battered, sad-looking U-Hauls.

I decided early on not to let their impermanence prevent me from becoming friends. I aimed to create memories and grasp tangible joys from these transient relationships, extracting what I could before another good-bye was foisted upon me. I was adept at making friends and getting close fast, because I never knew what could be learned before the leave-takings of the wondrous mix of women hailing from various parts of the world.

The need to prepare my heart for eventual absences was never far from the potluck gatherings at church, Friday mornings at playgroup, chats, and playdates. Yes, losing friends who moved away still hurt, some more than others, depending on the level our friendship had taken. I did have one weapon in my arsenal that kept me from staying bereft and long faced when yet another special person passed through: I loved to write letters. That sustained me for many years, making the breaks not so final and drastic at the time.

Standing at the door very soon after the new family moved in, my three children and I delivered a plate of chocolate chip cookies, a courtesy we tried to perform for everyone moving onto our block on Franklin Street. Nothing extraordinary stood out or signaled anything momentous. If only neon signs had proclaimed, "She's going to be special. She's going to be special. Wait and see." But they didn't. We merely smiled at each other during our initial meet and greet, while our combined five children shyly gazed at each other.

That simple welcome proved a pivotal moment in both our lives. Mary Kenyon and I just didn't know it yet.

It didn't take long before a fledgling friendship took wing, since Mary and I had so much in common. We were stay-at-home moms with BA degrees in our background. We grew up in large Catholic families (I was the oldest of eight; she was the seventh of ten). We breastfed our babies and toddlers beyond socially approved norms. We loved to read and write. She joined the weekly playgroup I coordinated at my church. And Mary rejuvenated my interest in couponing and refunding to an entirely new level, since money was always tight for our one-income families.

Our four older children naturally gravitated toward each other, rapidly using up the sidewalk between our homes. My Jill and her Danny, both six years old, were born just a couple weeks apart. Our Elizabeths, aged four, had mere months separating them. My youngest, two-year-old Jonathan, while the odd man out, still managed to work in some playing action with his sisters and new neighbors.

Mary and I spent so much time together that it seemed like the Kenyon family lived on Franklin Street for at least two to three years, if not more. I believed this until Mary commented that it had only been one year. What? Only one? Impossible.

So how did we maintain our friendship after Mary moved from the neighborhood? By writing letters. Yes, that's right. Good old hand-written letters. Lots and lots of them. Unlike some relationships where pen-palling waxed and waned, there was no waning with us.

Our friendship blossomed through hundreds, then thousands, of letters in the ensuing years. As our relationship deepened, I noticed she rarely mentioned other females besides her sisters.

During that time, my children grew older, needed me less, and eventually moved on to college. I joined several women's clubs and organizations, building foundations with a variety of women of all ages, many who to this day bless me with their presence in my life. How many are there? Honestly, I don't know, but one thing is clear: I take none of them for granted. Each one provides a unique luster to my life.

Inevitably, my letters to Mary detailed the multitude of activities that graced my life. I attended board meetings, luncheons, special church activities, writing groups, and Bible studies, and I made road trips to visit out-of-town friends and family. I noticed she didn't do the same.

It was only years later when our face-to-face visits became more frequent that she would divulge the reason for her difficulty in making friends. I was shocked to learn about the bullying she endured in elementary school, and how even as an adult, it took courage for her to walk into a room full of women.

An Unexpected Pairing

Kathy Millikan

Who would have guessed that as I flipped through the pages of *Liguorian* magazine all those years ago, I was about to embark on an amazing journey of friendship that has continued for nearly thirty years?

It started out innocently enough . . . basic, simple, straightforward. I was a young mother looking for information regarding starting a playgroup for my two little ones. Mary Humston had recently written an article in *Liguorian* that caught my attention. I decided to write and ask about the realities and how-tos of starting and maintaining a playgroup.

Her answer came back quickly. She was eager to share her knowledge. And yet, on some level, it still seemed odd to be corresponding with someone I knew so little about. I ventured to ask her some personal questions, and she wrote back with queries of her own. Questions asked and answered with actual pen-on-paper letters . . . that even required stamps. Cards, too—I am an avid card-sender, and I'm sure that, over the years, Mary has learned that when she receives a card with a California postmark, addressed in colored ink, and covered with stickers appropriate to the occasion, she needs to open it very carefully, because it will be filled with shiny confetti. We didn't realize it at the time, but we were on a trajectory that would take us many letters and years into the future.

Since we had so much in common, we were never lacking newsy tidbits to fill our handwritten pages. We were both young moms, women of faith, and, to put the icing on the cake, avid tea drinkers. In fact, Mary is involved with several teas held at her church each year. I host an annual Christmas tea in my home for my Bible study group and a

Valentine's Day tea, a more intimate get-together with my close circle of friends. I also enjoy visiting and discovering different tearooms throughout Southern California and farther afield when I am traveling.

For as many commonalities as we shared, there were just as many differences. Mary is a Midwest farm girl from Iowa. I am a native Californian. Snow, ice, and freezing temperatures are not in my vocabulary; beach, ocean, and sand are not in hers. And yet we clicked.

As the years went by, and our precious little ones matured into teenagers, we became prayer partners too (it's funny how the prayer time increases exponentially during the teen years). Via snail mail, we flung prayer requests back and forth—the United States Post Office had no idea what kind of a role it was playing in the spiritual lives of our two families. We knew we could have just picked up the phone and called each other at any time. But there seemed to be an unwritten, unspoken rule that we both understood: the phone was taboo. Although, over the years, I have to admit I was truly tempted to break that rule a few times, but there was something about the written word.

We have never even resorted to the modern-day convenience of email, which was in its infancy when our correspondence began. Unbelievably, in 2013, the opportunity arose for us to meet face-to-face. Mary's daughter was attending a conference in California, and, as fate would have it, Mary was coming with her to care for her infant granddaughter who was still breastfeeding. Mary did some logistical homework and figured out this might be as close as we would ever get to each other (of course we "discussed" it through frequent trips back and forth to our respective mailboxes). But as the day of our first meeting approached, texts and even phone calls were exchanged.

Imagine how strange it was—until that first call, we didn't even know what the other sounded like. It was a bit like a first date in that we didn't quite know what to expect. But looking back, how silly we were to be anxious. For heaven's sake, we'd been writing, baring our souls, for over twenty years.

There is always a measure of uncertainty upon meeting someone for the first time, but really, the connection was already there. I knew what she looked like—we had exchanged pictures over the years—plus, she would be the one pushing the stroller around the lobby. We shared lunch and a lovely afternoon accompanied by Mary's granddaughter Zoey (actually, she was our little icebreaker and a delightful companion). As naturally as with two women who had been friends for decades, our conversation picked up where our letters left off. And when it was time to leave, we were completely comfortable. It was as if we had known each other forever, which of course we had.

Kathy Millikan lives in Diamond Bar, California, with her husband of nearly thirty-five years, Kevin. She has four children and three grandchildren. She co-leads a weekly women's Bible study and enjoys reading, baking, walking (off those cookies), and date nights with her husband.

CHAPTER TWO

Mothers

Dear Mary, did your mother
have female friends?

Mary Potter Kenyon

My father was my mother's best friend. In fact, as far as I could tell while growing up, he seemed to be her only friend. Perhaps it wasn't always this way. Maybe older or younger siblings remember differently, but I have no memory of my mother having a female confidante while she raised us. I never knew her to talk on the phone, go out for lunch or shopping, share a cup of coffee, or spend any time with other women.

I do remember her calling out a greeting to the neighbor across the fence when she hung out laundry, but I also recall what happened when Mom invited her over once. Even as a preteen, it was clear to me that this woman looked down on us. Her pinched look as she surveyed her surroundings revealed her disdain for the "poor family" next door. It didn't help that she criticized my mother for not allowing us to drink the Kool-Aid her daughters drank liberally. "It's really cheap," she pushed, but Mom held steadfast to her notion that powdered milk was better for us. Which, of course, it was.

What my mother lacked in face-to-face communication, she made up for in the copious amount of letters she wrote to her parents, aunts, uncles, cousins, and—from the looks of the address book I inherited after her death—anyone she came across in her limited travels. I found it unusual, and somewhat touching, that her address book contained names and addresses of seatmates on the buses that took her to visit my younger sisters after Dad's death. What I didn't find, however, were names of personal friends, outside of those few she discovered late in life.

This makes me sad now, though I accepted it without question while growing up. Her eyes would brighten when she talked about her high school friend Beverly. I know she made at least some effort to reconnect with old friends and classmates at a fifty-year class reunion, but it was the men she came home talking about, one in particular whom she visited several times on the way to see her mother. By then, she'd been widowed long enough she might have considered herself available, though she'd often declared she would never find a man to love like she'd loved our father.

Did she ever yearn for a friend when she was a young mother? Did she even care for women in general? "I always liked men better than women," she'd often mused.

Perhaps her example could partially explain my own problems in forming and maintaining friendships beyond high school. Or maybe it was that neither of us had time or money to cultivate them. Go out to lunch? My parents didn't do date night or eat out. The only place I knew them to go alone was the grocery store.

I know my mother formed a few friendships after my father's death in 1986. There was the widow who lived across the railroad tracks who often asked for rides to appointments. But when Mom was diagnosed with lung cancer in the summer of 2010, she was hesitant to tell this woman.

"She'll say 'I told you so' about my smoking," my mother worried. It broke my heart that she was ashamed about her diagnosis, and it hurt even more that she would think someone would be so unkind. Would a true friend say such a thing? Hadn't this same woman visited Mom after Dad's death, throwing open the curtains and declaring that it was time she began living again? Wouldn't she encourage Mom in this, too?

"She won't say that. Not if she is really your friend." I encouraged her to call.

Unfortunately, my mother's fears were well founded. "I told you so" is exactly what the woman said. As far as I know, that comment ended the friendship.

Another friend of sorts was a distant relative who had written Mom for years, seeking spiritual advisement and trusting her with confidences

about a troubled marriage and family. "Spiritual adviser" was a role my
mother took seriously. I was at Mom's house when this "friend" visited
her during her last weeks.

"Well, what did you expect after all your years of smoking?" she
scolded. I was glad for my mother's radiation-induced deafness and the
woman's soft voice when the comment wasn't acknowledged.

She gestured to me. "I don't think your mother is hearing anything
I'm saying."

Confusion crossed her face when I replied, "Good," and quickly
changed the subject.

This same woman later emailed me for the advice she'd once counted
on from Mom. "Your mother had always said you were closest to her in
your religious beliefs," she explained.

My email reply was swift: "If you want me to tell you the same thing
my mother would nave, and give you permission to skip your grandson's
wedding because he isn't being married in the Catholic Church, you
will be sorely disappointed. My advice is to go. Go to your grandson's
non-Catholic wedding, or at least his reception if you can't bring yourself
to set foot inside another church. Don't make the mistake my mother
made and potentially hurt your relationship with a family member with
the misguided notion that you are sinning by attending. Your grandson
will never forget his grandmother missing this special day."

I never heard from her again.

I am glad my mother seemed to have discovered one true friend from
her church in her later years. Gloria was a younger version of herself: long
hair and skirts, and a dozen children straggling after her to the pew each
Sunday. I admit to being a little jealous of the relationship between Gloria
and my mother. I noted the wistful tone whenever she talked about her
young friend, revealing a keen disappointment in her own daughters who
did not fit the mold of the devout Catholic. I always felt as though I had
failed Mom by not being more like Gloria.

Gloria did not judge my mother for her diagnosis or criticize her for smoking. She simply loved her. She was one of the few people who allowed her to smoke in the house when she had her over for lunch or coffee. She visited Mom as she lay on her deathbed, bringing copies of the prayers she knew Mom would have wanted us to pray. She knelt and led a Rosary. Gloria was a good friend. In the end, outside of family, she may have been my mother's only real friend.

"You only need one true friend," Mom always said. She had that at the end of her life.

Mary Jedlicka Humston

When Mary wrote her portion of this chapter, she had to rely on memories and old letters. I am fortunate to live only twenty minutes from my mom, Irene Kathryn Leonard Jedlicka, who is eighty-two years old. With tape recorder in tow, my husband, Jim, and I drove to Mom and Dad's home. While he and Dad visited in the living room, Mom and I settled into soft kitchen chairs. Because Mary and I thought it best to retain Mom's story in her own words, we decided to keep it in the interview format. Here is a condensed version of our conversation from February 4, 2015.

Mary: We're going to talk about your friendships throughout the years. Tell me about the first friends you remember as a kid.

Mom: Well, I remember when I was around five years old, there was a girl named Nancy in Johnny's [my older brother's] grade. She and I used to sit around in the ditches at school where we could watch everyone else playing. Nancy died when her mother was making popcorn and the stove caught fire. I remember we went to her funeral. I remember that very well. She had a younger sister, Marilyn, who later on became one of my very closest friends. Another friend was Marjana, the youngest of eight girls in a family of nine children. We three used to stay overnight at each other's houses. We didn't get together much because in those days, you didn't go over and play like today. It was a long way to go, so you'd just see them at school, play with them, and eat lunch together.

So if you had to figure out who were your first friends, would they have been cousins or would they have been kids at school?

We didn't get to see our cousins hardly ever because that was during World War II. There was a gas shortage. After the war was over, we did see our cousins a little more.

You see, that's interesting to me, because I just assumed mobility would be easy. But to just travel and to get in the car was limited then?

It certainly was. Grandpa might've gotten a little bit more gas rations by being a farmer and owning a pickup, but we did not get to go around and visit relatives until Bill and Lena [my aunt and uncle] moved in not too far from where Grandma and Grandpa lived. Then I spent time with their daughter Carol, but she was way younger.

In the days when you didn't have to worry about the gas shortage, did Grandma and Grandpa have a lot of friends?

Oh, yes, they did. And Grandma took people in. The cousins would come out from Chicago and stay at our house. Maybe some old aunt would spend the summer. There were always people there.

When did you go to Catholic school? Did you have trouble making friends? What did you and your friends do for fun?

I started there in eighth grade. I was the new kid, but it didn't matter. They just treated me so nicely. That was a wonderful place to go. It was always easy to make friends.

By then, the war was over, so we could go to ball games. We went to a lot of the away games. We only had basketball. We didn't have any other sports. We had school dances. And we'd eat lunch with other boys and girls from my grade. We always ate together.

It must've been easy for you to make friends, because you were the homecoming queen. I mean, you obviously had good relationships with a lot of people.

Yeah, I think everybody liked me. I was okay. [We both laugh.]

I think so, too. Well then, when you went to nursing school, did you live at home or did you live on campus? What kinds of things did you do with friends then?

We were required to live on campus. I lived in a dorm by Mercy Hospital [Iowa City]. I always had nice roommates, but the primary thing there was to make good grades. If we didn't, we washed out very quickly. Usually we were assigned a roommate. I always had two to my room. Some rooms had four girls, which is quite a few when trying to study, but we could go off and study elsewhere, like to the library. I was there for three years. All summer long, too. Very intense studying. It would take most of the kids nowadays probably four years to do what we did in three.

For fun, we could go get a hamburger and a Coke up at the Hamburg Inn, which was close by.

What was the name of your nursing friend who later moved to Florida? You kept in touch with her all those years by writing letters, right? That's what's interesting about our book: the whole aspect of letter writing. You probably didn't call much back then, did you?

Yes, we kept in touch through letters. You didn't use the phone. You paid dearly to make a call in those days. That was—oh gosh, that was just something almost sacred, to make a call on my parents' phone. Shirley would visit often in the summers because her family was up here, her parents and brothers and sisters.

Did that ability to make friends or the opportunity to make friends change once you started having all of us kids? How did that work? I don't remember you going out to lunch with friends.

I think the friends just became different people who also had children. No, I never went to lunch. We didn't have time, actually, because I would've had to feed all you kids before I ever went. Plus, I'd have to get someone to watch you all. No, I never went out anyplace really. It was pretty much stay at home. There was so much to do. Canning, and chickens, and so much to provide all the food. Until Amy started school, I didn't go hardly anywhere. At that time it didn't seem like any deprivation. It just wasn't the way it could be. We did what we had to do, and that's the way it was.

So it wasn't something you regretted not having, because you knew you couldn't do it?

No, no, I never regretted it, because I could see Esther and Leona and other people in the same boat. They didn't get to go anywhere either.

What do you do with your friends now?

Friends are the people from church or the people I worked with. We [the ladies who worked in the elementary-school lunchroom] do go and have coffee once a month.

And now do you feel the need for a best friend?

Not really. I'm with Dad all the time.

Would you consider him your best friend?

Oh, yeah. He always has been.

We've talked about your first friends at country school, what you did, when you went to the Catholic school, nursing school, friends you had while you parented us. What about the Altar & Rosary Society at St. Mary's Newport Church?

Oh, that was nice. We met every month at our homes and said the Rosary. And then we did some good works. We might sew for some place like the Tommy Dale Memorial Hospital in Sioux City. We would do whatever would be helpful. We didn't meet in the summer, though we met all the rest of the time. That was all the while we were out at Newport Church.

Also, the Altar & Rosary up here [in Solon]. I help with all the funeral dinners. I don't go and work anymore, but I send food, and they're all nice people.

Do you have any final thoughts about the importance of friends?

I always wondered what it would be like to have a sister, but you can't always have what you want. I always thought that would be a very special bond. The brothers were nice, but that's just one thing I've thought of occasionally, but not too much, because you can't control that.

I will always cherish the memory of having this conversation in the comfort of Mom's kitchen with the soft murmur of Jim's and Dad's voices in the background. I learned many things about Mom. One of the biggest surprises was that she lost her friend, Nancy, in a deadly fire. I can't even imagine what that must've been like for a very young child to experience. I also hadn't taken into account the effects of World War II on school activities and visiting with relatives. Three years of nursing school also surprised me. I'd thought it had only been one. Perhaps I'll interview Mom again someday. And this time include Dad, too. Who knows what I might learn?

Thirty Years of Ink and Paper

Mary Neville, Marlene Neville, and Amber Neville

Mary:

Being a mother-in-law sometimes doesn't bring the best thoughts to mind. We have all heard the jokes; however, for me it has been great. Soon after my son and his wife were married, they moved across the state to Iowa City. This could have been the end of family closeness except that my daughter-in-law is a wonderful correspondent.

Each week, sometimes twice a week, she wrote a letter telling about the events in their lives, big and small. This was a time before technology was going strong, so letter writing was the best way to stay in touch, and stamps were less expensive than a phone call. It was very meaningful to know about new friends being made and recipes tried and to hear the details as grandchildren arrived and grew up.

Since I'm a saver, I kept all those letters and eventually returned them to my first granddaughter to read, save, or pass on.

In the years since, computers have become popular, and my daughter-in-law continues to keep me caught up on their family activities. (It is difficult for me to say "daughter-in-law" because I really consider her my second daughter.) What a blessing her letters, and now emails, are to me.

Marlene:

After my husband and I moved from northwest Iowa to Iowa City, I found myself suddenly very isolated from my family. We didn't have the instant gratification of communication that we experience today, except for a telephone, and that was expensive. That is when I began writing letters to my parents and my husband's parents. I would write at least once a week, if not two or three times. These letters would hold descriptions of our weather, fun times with friends we had made, our little ups and downs, and anything else I thought would interest them. I wanted our extended families to be a part of our daily lives, and so our lives were documented in these weekly letters.

The journeys recorded in these letters included the anticipation of the arrival of our three children and all their milestones, the trials and tribulations of being parents, fun times and sad times we experienced as a family, and daily life as we knew it.

These letters expanded over a thirty-year period. Little did I know, my husband's mother saved each and every one of them, pages and pages documenting our lives. And even more special was that she bundled them all up and passed those thirty years of our life on to my oldest daughter shortly after she gave birth to her first daughter.

These letters were a thread that connected lives. By reading them, we can relive over and over the life experiences and emotions that they hold.

Amber:

I have a box of letters, all gathered into neat bundles. They were written to my grandmother from my mother, and a few are from my father. They span a considerable time, almost thirty years, and they are brimming with the many small details that make up daily life. I love them.

These letters are a direct physical link with the past. In my mom's own swooping handwriting, I can read about my shockingly young parents and their first apartment in town, the excitement over their first pregnancy (me!), trips, jobs, friends, car trouble, new sandals, weather, more babies, new homes, and dinner parties. They hold wonderful little anecdotes about my parents' life with small and growing children, particularly intriguing to me as I have my own small children now.

I like to think about my mom sitting at the kitchen table writing them and my grandma picking them up at the post office and reading them aloud to my grandpa. It's so easy to see this weekly ritual. My mom stopped writing letters around the time that I graduated from high school and entered college—coinciding, more or less, with the arrival of email.

Letter writing has largely gone out of style; it's too slow, too time consuming. That's true, of course. Email is superior in speed and efficiency, but I'm so glad I have those neat bundles of letters. I get to hold some of my family's past right there in my hands. I'll keep them for my own children to read someday. I can imagine how fascinating each folded sheet will be to them, those rare and precious treasures from the past.

Mary Hal (Nance) Neville was born August 7, 1928, in Graham, Texas, to Alfred Harold Nance and Mary Anna (Warren) Nance. She graduated from Graham High School in 1945. Mary attended college at North Texas State University in Denton, Texas. She married Russell Leroy Neville on February 1, 1947, and moved to Iowa. Mary has three children, six grandchildren, and seven great-grandchildren.

Marlene Neville was born in Walton, New York, in the heart of the Catskill Mountains. She grew up on a dairy farm, where she wrote and received many letters. She now is a dental assistant living in Iowa City with Michael, her husband of almost forty years. Marlene has two daughters, one son, three granddaughters, and one grandson.

Amber Neville is a librarian who lives in Iowa City, Iowa, with her husband and two children. She loves to read and to travel with her family.

CHAPTER THREE

Mean Girls

Dear Mary, did you have friends when
you were growing up?

Mary Potter Kenyon

"Mary, do you know who I am? You went to school with my sister."

I was at a salon having my hair done for an event where I would be the featured speaker when the woman approached my chair. I was instantly thrust back to my elementary years and the meanness of her sister. In my mind's eye, I saw the girl's sneer and watched the spittle from her mouth hit my arm. I felt the shove into a wall. I heard her trademark phrase: "Ewww . . . Potter."

"Patty" was the epitome of the "mean girl" at the Catholic school I attended for six years. She was instrumental in making grade school a living hell. While she was not the only one who bullied me, she was the worst and the most relentless. Her sister, however, had always been kind to me. She couldn't have known the torment her younger sibling inflicted on me—a torment that evidently lay just beneath the surface of my soul even as an adult. Here I was, forty-three years later, still hurting as if it were yesterday.

Until I went to school, I had never thought of myself as poor. In fact, it was a casual comment from a first-grade classmate that clued me in. Pointing up, the girl at the bottom of a stairwell had remarked to a friend, "There's the poor girl." Startled, I'd looked behind me, but no one else was there.

It speaks highly of my parents that, until that day, I had never realized that my family lived in poverty. That naivety also meant I was an easy target, a shy girl who had been sheltered inside a loving home from the cruelty of the outside world. When I began school, it never occurred to me it might be a place to make friends. I was there because I had to be there in order to learn to read and write like my older siblings. I had plenty of playmates at home.

However, it wasn't long before I saw the advantage to having friends. I had no one to play with at recess, no one to pick me for a team, and no one who would stand up to Patty. There were girls who never participated in the bullying but were likely scared to be associated with me. Someone would bravely befriend me for a day or two, and my heart would soar with the unexpected kindness. But not even the bravest dared to face the wrath of Patty on the warpath, and for whatever reason, I was her chosen target. Boys were mean enough, tripping me and shoving me in the hallway, but at least they were consistently mean. How could I trust a girl who one day offered kindness only to turn away the next? I learned I could trust no female.

School rules perpetuated the difference in socioeconomic status between the poor children there on scholarship and the rich little Catholic girls. Instead of being sent out for recess after lunch, the children who couldn't afford meal tickets were forced to clean off tables and do the dishes. The requirement of having to wear dresses also drew attention to those who couldn't afford nice clothes. The other girls wore one of a dozen puffed-sleeved frocks with their white bobby socks and shiny white or black patent leather shoes. I had perhaps a single dress each year, maybe a skirt and blouse, and wore boys' brown shoes with utilitarian, thick knee-socks that were held up with rubber bands. The skirts often sported a faded crease where a hem had been let down. My first bra in sixth grade was a sister's stretched-out hand-me-down held together by a large safety pin. The only time we were allowed to wear pants underneath our skirts was when the temperature was subzero. I didn't own pants or snow boots, so I wore a pair of my brother's white work pants along with my mother's clear galoshes. It is no wonder I was made fun of. My motley wardrobe practically begged for it. The constant odors of wood and cigarette smoke that clung to my hair and clothing probably didn't help either.

Ironically, while my parents struggled mightily to send their children to parochial elementary school, it wasn't until I attended public school in seventh grade that I escaped the bowels of my own private hell.

I had no idea what to expect in a larger school, and I worried that seventh grade would be even worse because of an increase in potential tormentors. Instead, the action of a single girl changed my life trajectory. Annette Nieman will forever remain high on my pedestal. The pretty, bespectacled blonde, already popular among her public school peers, sidled up to me on the first day of junior high and welcomed me to the new school. Perhaps it was the fact that we were two of the more well-endowed seventh graders, or maybe she saw my deer-in-the-headlights look and took pity. Whatever it was, that day marked a change in my school experiences.

As Annette and I strolled down the hallway, arm in arm, we met fellow Catholic school transplant Patty walking alone from the other direction.

"Ewwww . . . Pot . . . " Patty's voice trailed off and her mouth hung open as her eyes darted nervously from me to the blonde goddess. She was at a loss as to what to do since she'd never seen me accompanied in a hallway before. She looked down at the ground and hurried away. We didn't exchange a single word for the next six years of school. When she sent me a friend request on Facebook some forty years later, I couldn't bring myself to respond.

Annette was the first of many friends I developed in junior high and high school. Thanks to a babysitting job that allowed for a few new clothing purchases and several excellent teachers who encouraged me in writing, art, and drama, I gained enough confidence to join clubs and participate in after-school activities. I wrote for the newspaper, won many awards, was inducted into the National Honor Society, and even played the lead part of Dorothy in the high school production of *The Wizard of Oz*. All of these experiences brought me situational friendships, at least: girls who were also in speech or drama or who wrote for the newspaper. But as much fun as I had with some of them, our friendships didn't stand the test of time. Other than an occasional letter and visit, I basically had remained friendless until the day I met Mary.

Mary Jedlicka Humston

uilding friendships as a youngster was painless, because my siblings were immediate playmates. As the oldest, I was eight and a half years old when child number seven arrived. No, that's not a typo. In that time period, Mom birthed seven children—with, I might add, no twins. When I was a high school senior, child number eight, Amy, was born, nine years after the seventh child, Julie. Amy turned nine months old when I headed to college as a seventeen-year-old farm girl, probably one of the few freshmen with a baby sister.

In the 1960s, when we kids weren't helping with chores, butchering and dressing chickens, gathering eggs from the chicken coop, canning and freezing vegetables and fruits with Mom, pulling weeds in the garden, and performing other sundry farm duties, we played. We found hours of outdoor fun in exploring the timbers, the creek, our many acres of land, the large farmyard, and our fenced-in house yard. We rode old bikes on our three-quarter-mile lane, climbed trees in the orchard, jumped around on bales in the haymow, and interacted with a bevy of farm cats and dogs.

We also invented games. We older girls spent hours playing with models we cut from the pages of the Montgomery Ward or Sears catalogs. Called "ladies," they became our paper dolls. I always named mine, writing first and last names on the back of each one, and grouped them into families that interacted with each other.

Having ready-made playmates did one thing: it bonded us. To this day, I am privileged to count my four sisters and three brothers (and their spouses) as friends.

Since large families were common back then, it's no surprise I had numerous first cousins. Cousin Linda, the third child out of ten, was two years older than I and lived on a farm approximately thirty miles south of us. Patty, the fourth of five kids, was born a month after me. Now called Pat, she grew up a farm girl who ended up a town kid in a county north of us. Their friendships remain precious to me, despite time and distance making visits few and far between.

Karen was another close friend. She was the oldest child of Mom and Dad's longtime friends Betty and Gerald. Their eight children were either born in the same year or were in the same grade as us Jedlicka siblings except for the last child in each family. Though they lived over thirty-five miles from us, I remember many gatherings at their farm or ours.

I'm probably one of few Iowans my age who attended a one-room school. What an experience! I went to Coon Creek Country School near Sutliff, Iowa, from first grade to the middle of fifth grade. And, my goodness, we walked seven miles each way, sometimes in ten-foot snowdrifts during winter . . . just kidding. My grade included two boys and two girls (except when another girl came for just one year). Making friends wasn't complicated when there were approximately fourteen students in the entire school.

I lost track of my first school friend, Cheri, but I cherish many memories of her. As fourth graders, we joined an enraptured television audience when the Beatles performed on the Ed Sullivan Show. We played Barbies for hours. While swimming in her plastic pool one summer, I broached the profound question: "Hey, would anyone know if we went to the bathroom in here?" Her mother's "Don't do it!" carried loudly from the nearby kitchen window.

When Dad and Mom bought their first farm and we moved, country school days ended. Walking into Solon Elementary School, where the fifth-grade classes numbered nearly fifty students, had to be my first experience with sensory overload. A single room seemed almost as big as Coon Creek. Everyone stared at me, the new girl, the suddenly shy girl. I sunk into my assigned chair, lost in the swelling abundance of kids.

Pamela was assigned to show me around and help me acclimate, yet I still didn't know how to act in this large school, and I especially didn't know how to navigate the shrieking, raucous recesses with ten times the number of pieces of playground equipment than Coon Creek had. Students from several classrooms crowded and mingled together. Who should I play with? How did I go about making a friend? Who did I choose? Girls? Or boys? Did they choose me? I quickly learned making friends took effort. They didn't instantly materialize like they had at home, family gatherings, or country school. Eventually, I gravitated to a few girls during those later elementary and junior high years, but shyness and insecurity remained.

I was so shy and insecure that hearing the words "Gee, you're fat" once thrust me into the fallacy of "sticks and stones may break my bones, but words shall never harm me." I don't recall anyone at school ever speaking to me like that before. There was nowhere to run from those three humiliating words while sitting in junior high music class. The accompanying sneer made them more potent. Real. True. As a husky adolescent, I sheltered that denigrating phrase deep within me and never told another soul, not even my sister Kathy, my friends, or my mom. I couldn't. I was sure I had to be disgustingly fat. Why else would a classmate—who rarely, if ever, talked to me—have said so?

Anorexia wasn't a commonly used term back in the late 1960s, but "Gee, you're fat" propelled me into another world where I vowed I'd never hear those words directed at me again. Leggy, thin models graced magazine covers, perpetuating a thin-is-in society. It didn't take long to shed that "fat" image down to 104 pounds. A distorted body image plagued me for years, but, thankfully, anorexia health problems didn't swallow me up as they could have.

The summer before becoming a freshman in high school in the late 1960s, I worked on the outer me. I indeed lost weight and exercised voraciously, running down the lane and through the hills long before jogging became a craze. Upon the advice of one of my friends, I let my chin-length straight hair grow into the up-and-coming style of that hippie decade. It eventually reached my waist and stayed there for years.

Learning to sew most of my clothes boosted my self-esteem. A limited wardrobe in junior high spurred me toward learning to make my own jackets, vests, culottes, two prom dresses, a velvet homecoming mini-dress, hot pants (!), and many other pieces thanks to my mom, who could read any puzzling pattern or get me out of a stitched mess when seams and darts didn't materialize accurately.

Having addressed my physical appearance, I then had the courage to address my shyness, especially my tongue-tied behavior around boys. Freshman year began with the intention to start conversations with others. "You had a good answer in class today." "Nice dress." "Great game last night." While not easy, it gradually became more comfortable.

I joined the newspaper staff and later switched to yearbook. I was a cheerleader all four years, three of them on varsity, two of those as captain. Induction into the National Honor Society came as a sophomore. When I was voted homecoming queen and student council president my senior year, I knew I'd come a long way. Yet those awkward days of junior high are still cemented deep within me: the days of minimal wardrobe, acne, makeup and hair issues, body image problems, and low self-esteem.

Making changes and approaching others in high school had far-reaching impacts. The main one was finding I had a knack for making friends. That ability would come in handy as a mother of young children in a college town when meeting new friends happened frequently.

From Five to Eighty-Five: Friendship to Last a Lifetime

Jill L. Humston and Rebecca "Becky" L. Reese

What is your earliest memory of us together?

Becky:

I remember several things from afternoon kindergarten with Mrs. Daters at Mark Twain Elementary. You used to call me at home every morning before school to find out what I was going to wear, so that you could try to wear something similar. How's that for closeness? I would often go to your house after school since your parents lived very close, and I enjoyed your mom's chocolate chip cookies and grape juice before I headed home.

Jill:

My mom still makes you a special plate of chocolate chip cookies when you are back in Iowa. Now your husband, Murat, enjoys them, too. I can't wait for the newest member of your family, Evren, to try them when he is old enough to eat solid foods.

One of my first memories was also in kindergarten. We had gotten out early from school due to a snow and ice storm. We had to walk down a small incline from the building to cross the street, then walk four houses down the block to get to my parents'. We were both so scared of slipping and falling. We were holding hands and crying. The crossing guard was your brother's friend, and he helped us across the street. We crawled all the rest of the way home. It seems so overdramatic now, but felt quite traumatic at the time. I would still crawl through ice with you.

Becky:

That same memory is vivid for me as well. It sounds silly now, but I re-member that intense fear of falling on the ice. We didn't know it at the time, but that was the first of many times we would see each other through a difficult or scary situation.

What makes our friendship unique from others?

Becky:

One thing that makes our bond unique is the sheer amount of time we've known each other and one another's families. You knew my mother, who passed away several years ago, only five years fewer than I did. Because of that, you knew what she was like when we were little, what types of things she might cook for dinner, and how she would entertain us when we had sleepovers at my house. In that sense, you help me to remember and honor my mother in a way that few of my friends are able to do. Each year on the anniversary of my mom's passing, you send a card or other-wise reach out.

Jill:

So many of my childhood memories include you, and in that way, they include your mom as well. I can still hear her voice, how she answered the phone or laughed with us. My son, Asher, is almost as old as we were when we met. Watching him and his friends together makes me realize we were probably quite a riot for her, as well as for my parents. I often think of you as more like a sister or my favorite cousin than I do as just my friend. I don't call my sister every day or even every week. You and I don't talk on the phone often either, but I know that we are there for one another. We've been a constant factor in each other's lives for nearly our whole lives, and that is very special.

What has helped us maintain our friendship over the years?

Becky:

Despite not always being able to communicate or visit as often as would be ideal, we have such a rich shared history, which serves as a strong foundation for our relationship. We know implicitly that we value each other immensely, and we care deeply about what's happening to the other person. Because of this history, we also have a kind of shared language, or a way of communicating that is unique to us.

Jill:

Communication has been key. We have had so many important and serious conversations. These have occurred since very early in our child-hood and defined critical steps in our development as people. We share many of the same ideas and values on family and on healthy lifestyles. We have supported each other in the decision-making process on everything from love and relationships to a commitment to education and careers. Even early in high school, we knew what we wanted to do with our lives. Grades and education were important to us. We helped each other strive to make our goals a reality. We studied together for Mr. Muilenburg's physical science class as freshmen and Mr. Wilson's chemistry class as juniors. I helped you learn calculus in college. Then we both entered doctoral programs. Incidentally, you chose Washington University in St. Louis after you visited me there one summer while I was doing an internship. So I indirectly take credit for you meeting your husband during graduate school. We have always had plenty to talk about, especially now that we are both raising little boys.

What are some challenges we have faced?

Becky:

Probably the biggest challenge is geographical distance. In college, we were only a 1.5-hour drive apart, so we were able to get together frequently, which was wonderful. But after that, we each moved out of Iowa to attend doctoral programs, which meant that we spent much less time together. As each of us matured, individuated, and formed new support networks, we did not always get together or talk on the phone as much as we might have liked. But we quickly noticed that as soon as we did see each other again, it would be as if no time at all had passed.

Jill:

I agree. I always loved the way you introduced me or talked about me with your St. Louis graduate school crew. There was always "my best friend, Summer, and my oldest friend, Jill."

As busy professionals, it is hard to stay in touch, but we know that the other is always just a text or phone call away. We only see each other a couple of times a year, but that effort to see each other is a given. There isn't really a question of *if*, it's just *when*.

What is your favorite memory of us?

Becky:

There are so many to choose from. I would have to narrow it to two—one happy and one not so happy. One of my happiest, more recent memories is from my wedding in 2010. You, your mom and dad, your husband, Andrew, and newborn, Asher, were at my wedding in St. Louis even though you had just given birth a mere four weeks before. I was thrilled that my oldest friend was able to participate in my big day, and having an itty-bitty baby there made for some great photographic moments. Today, having recently had my first child, I now realize what an enormous gesture it was that you attended with such a tiny infant.

Another touching memory occurred just after my mom passed. I was lucky enough to have enormous support from loved ones during this terrible time, but I still can remember the moment I saw you after my mom died. We were at another friend's house, and you approached me and gave me the biggest, warmest, most comforting hug. I will never forget it. I can recall sobbing and feeling so supported and comforted. There was something almost maternal in that hug. It was so powerful that I wrote about it in my journal at the time.

Jill:

I am so glad that I could be there for you at that moment. I do wish I could have been there for you more near the end of her life.

What's ahead for our friendship?

Jill:

We've shared in grief and in joy. We've celebrated our own graduations, doctoral thesis defenses, new jobs, new loves, bachelorette parties, weddings, and baby showers. When Evren was born last year, he was born into a ready-made group of "friend cousins." There are now six little people who belong to four of us whose friendships have lasted since junior high.

There are friends of my parents who came to my high school graduation party and wedding, people who have known me from the very beginning. I see that for us as well. We'll watch each other's children grow up, support each other as parents and someday attend the young ones' celebrations and weddings, and become the old crew partying at the next generation's achievements.

Becky:

That is such a wonderful image. How fun to consider the role that we will play in our children's lives. Perhaps someday we will be at one of our offspring's major life events, reminiscing about that time we wrote a book chapter about our friendship, and all the memories we've made since.

Jill L. Humston lives in Waterloo, Iowa, with her husband, Andrew Ackermann, and their sons, Asher and Orrin. Jill earned her PhD from the University of Wisconsin–Madison in 2007 and taught chemistry at the University of Northern Iowa for four years before moving to middle- and high-school science education in 2011. She is fascinated by nature, the world, and the universe—a curiosity she fosters in her students and in her children. Her sons are also picking up her enthusiasm for running and being outdoors. She hopes to complete her first marathon in 2015.

Rebecca "Becky" L. Reese grew up in Iowa City, Iowa, and earned her PhD in clinical psychology from Washington University in St. Louis. She worked for three years at the Boston VA Healthcare System until her husband Murat accepted a position at the University of Pittsburgh. Becky now works as a health psychologist in Pittsburgh. When not working or playing with her newborn son, Evren, Becky enjoys doing yoga, hiking, traveling internationally, and exploring Pittsburgh's restaurants, parks, and museums.

CHAPTER FOUR

Oh, Baby!

Dear Mary, was it difficult for you to nourish
friendships as a young mother?

Mary Potter Kenyon

"It broke my heart that you thought it would be a good idea if you locked your children out of the bathroom. I'd like to publish your article, but only if you end it with the realization that attachment-style parenting was a good thing for your marriage and you would never consider locking little ones out of a bathroom."

The editor's email response to my essay submission had me shaking my head. I wanted my piece published, but I wasn't about to change the conclusion to fit the editor's agenda.

Not long ago, I unearthed my old weekly engagement books dating back to 1990, when I was a thirty-year-old mother of four. Two things are evident from these abbreviated journals: I loved my children with all my heart, and being a mother was a difficult job most days. Parenting was particularly hard considering the intensity of my mothering style. In the span of twenty years' worth of journals, I would add an additional four children to our fray. Those daybooks with their brief notations do a pretty fair job of chronicling what it was like to care for a large brood.

After several hours of reading them, my breath quickened and my heart raced. Before I succumbed to an anxiety attack, I shoved them back into the cupboard. I telephoned my daughter Elizabeth. When she picked up and said hello, I heard a screech in the background along with an ominous crash.

"How do you do it?" I asked without preamble. "How do you handle three children underfoot all day and not go crazy?"

"Who said I'm not crazy?" she retorted with a laugh.

Whether it was the influence of a selfless mother, Dr. William Sears (the guru of attachment-style parenting), a martyr complex, or a combination of all of the above, I immersed myself in mothering. I spent the majority of the years between 1980 and 2005 caring for either an infant or toddler, and usually both. I breastfed eight children for a total of eighteen years, sometimes weaning one only months before another was born. I wore my children in slings or backpacks long before it was cool to do so, used cloth diapers, and practiced the *family bed*. I added homeschooling to my already-busy schedule in 1993. I was certain God had a sense of humor when he gave me my two most active and demanding babies at the tail end of my parenting venture when I was forty and forty-three.

While I might have escaped unscathed if I'd parented this way with fewer children, the sheer number of years I practiced attachment-style parenting took its toll on me and my spousal relationship. It wasn't until my husband's cancer diagnosis in 2006 that I began reclaiming the marriage and, later, the self.

For the most part, my babies were healthy and happy, and my marriage survived the intensity of my parenting style. Despite what that editor wanted me to conclude, I wouldn't deny the truth. If I could go back in time and do it all over again, I would, at the very least, lock the door when I used the bathroom. It would have been one small declaration that I was a person too.

I couldn't bear to continue to read my journals, because I was reliving a period that had been full of angst. The blunt truth was that caring for so many offspring was difficult. That might be an understatement. Raising a large family is a herculean endeavor, and I am no Hercules. There's no politically correct way to put this: at times, I thought I might go stark raving mad.

And yet, I have no regrets regarding the number of amazing and creative individuals I gave birth to. What I do regret is how hard I made it on myself. I'm not sure I would have known how to be a different mother, since I did the best I could in the only way I knew how. In hindsight, my advice to my younger self would be to share the load a little, learn to delegate, work harder at maintaining the marriage relationship, and, yes, lock that darn bathroom door.

Did I have friends during those years? I tried. I yearned for that old across-the-backyard-fence friend, where I could borrow a cup of sugar and we could drink coffee while our children played together. I enjoyed brief relationships based on proximity when we lived in married student housing while David and I took classes at the University of Northern Iowa. A communal backyard where Dan and Elizabeth (then Danny and Bessie) played meant a casual acquaintance with other mothers. None of those relationships were sustained after we moved, and we moved a lot: from married student housing in Cedar Falls to a farmhouse, then another duplex, a rental house, then back to a duplex again. We were in Iowa City for a single year, only to return to Cedar Falls. From there, we moved thirty-five miles east to Independence, then farther east to Manchester, next to rural Dyersville for ten years, and finally back to Manchester, where I now reside in the very first house we owned, after twenty-eight years of marriage. I was never anywhere long enough to grow or sustain a neighborly relationship, except for the one I'd forged with Mary.

On those rare occasions when I met someone with friend potential, there was my messy house or lack of time to consider. I attended college classes and worked part time until December 1988 when I gave birth to Rachel, my fourth. I picked up part-time work writing for a newspaper when she was a few years old. Through the years, I alternated between helping a husband establish a bookstore, writing essays and articles, and running a home business selling used books. There were always piles of books and boxes strewn throughout the house, not to mention the usual toys and infant paraphernalia. Then for a few years I was an eBay seller, adding even more to the mess. I wasn't convinced a friend was worth the effort or the hours it would have taken to clean my house for visits. By then, David and I didn't have time to actively work on our own relationship, much less add anyone else to the busy mix.

Besides, I always had my sisters. I could sit with Sharon for hours while our children played together in the early '80s, or drink coffee and nurse an infant with Angie in 1987 when my Michael and her Michelle were born the same year. Who needs friends when there are sisters?

Yet there remained a secret yearning inside my heart. What would it be like to share those same activities with a woman outside my family? To have someone to go to garage sales with, or girl talk with on the phone? A friend to commiserate with who would understand the constant interruption of children's voices on the other end? I didn't know, but there was always a part of me that wondered.

By the time I met Mary, I would have admitted there might be something to having a female friend, something I might be missing out on. Mary exposed me to such a world with a playgroup, the La Leche League, and Bible study. I got a fleeting glimpse of what life could be like in a world that was bigger than my own extended family. And then I moved away from it. I would go on to have five more children, becoming increasingly isolated. By 1997, I was the mother of six children, living in the country, and homeschooling. There was a period of nearly ten years when weeks would go by and the only human contact I would have, outside of a husband who worked forty hours a week and a house full of children, were casual encounters with the mailman and the butcher. Thank goodness for those letters from Mary.

I cared for my children and my home, wrote essays and articles, and worked at a home business. I rarely went anywhere outside of copious shopping sprees funded by coupon savings. I attended some family functions, but ditched others, convinced no one cared whether I or my large brood attended.

I didn't see what was happening because I was mired in it, too busy trying to maintain a semblance of order in my home. But looking back, I see it. The self-imposed exile from the human race was not good for me or for my children. Seclusion may have contributed to an increase in writing clips, but, emotionally, I'd returned to feeling like the pariah I'd once been in grade school. My isolation increased when I experienced classic symptoms of undiagnosed postpartum depression after the births of my last three babies.

My husband's cancer diagnosis in 2006 cracked the protective shell I'd built around my fragile self. Suddenly I had places I needed to go: the hospital for visits after David's surgery, his doctor's appointments, and chemotherapy sessions. The smiles and pats on my arm from kind nurses and the influx of genuine love and consideration from those around us opened my eyes to a world I'd been convinced no longer existed—one filled with good and caring people.

My husband's eyes had been opened as well. He saw for the first time how secluded his family had become and how unhappy his wife was. It was David who encouraged me to join a women's exercise class—cost be damned. Instead of reluctantly allowing me time for writing, he became my biggest supporter, noticing how much good a two-hour writing session did me. Once he'd recovered from cancer treatment, he watched the children on his days off so I could exercise or spend time writing at a restaurant or a library. As soon as an opportunity presented itself, we moved from the rented farmhouse back to town where civilization awaited.

It wasn't until the summer of 2011 that, thanks to the encouragement of my supportive spouse, I would attend my first writing workshop in Cedar Falls. My mother had passed away the year before, and I'd inherited her notebooks and unpublished manuscripts. I fancied I was going with her blessing, following the advice she'd left behind in her notes: "I want my children to utilize their God-given talents."

I was finally taking my writing seriously, intent on obtaining a publisher for the book I'd worked on in Mom's empty house all winter. I had no idea then I would also be meeting a room full of creative Christian women and would learn what it was to establish true female friends. That first writing workshop was where I met my mentor, Shelly Beach. She and several other women there became more than writing peers. For the first time in my adult life, I was meeting women and making true friends.

Mary Jedlicka Humston

My wise husband Jim knew not to talk too often about the freedom he possessed while working his typical twenty-four-hour shift at the fire station. When the structured duty day was over, his evenings were more relaxed while waiting for emergency calls. In my time-starved world of having a newborn, a toddler, and a preschooler, I was delirious with envy hearing about Jim's workouts, how he could read a newspaper in one sitting, and even the covetous privacy to attend to bathroom needs solo. Never mind he put his life on the line and needed to be rested and ready. In those if-only-I-had-that-kind-of-free-time days, I focused on what he had in spades and what I craved with a vengeance. Even a scrap of ten minutes seemed like a luxury. I looked with longing at the hours he had that I didn't. I longed for *me* time.

I have always relished alone time. In fact, it was like breathing to me: essential, necessary, life giving. Was this because I was the oldest of so many siblings? Nurtured in me because I grew up on a farm with acres of timber and farmland begging for exploration? Or was it just me? From a young farm girl to today, I flourished with free time. Without a doubt, I'm not the me I'm supposed to be without it.

To help myself understand the intricacies of life, I've kept a journal since I was nineteen years old. Most entries have been written when I was sad, frustrated, upset, angry, confused, trying to find a solution to a problem, or searching for meaning in various situations. Yes, there are multiple entries full of joy, peace, and goodwill, but if someone who didn't know me well read my journals from my early 24/7 mothering period, they would get a skewed vision.

Recently I pulled out the journals from my first six years of mothering. While reading them, I actually shed tears for the woman I was then.

Exhausted. Overwhelmed. Behind in housework. Behind in correspondence. Stretched to the max with very little spark left and minimal time to
renew, refresh, or reflect. Though unable to finish a book, newspaper, or
project in one sitting, I always managed to finish a cookie (or two, or four)
or a bowl of chips without interruption. Go figure.

Those journals are rife with the pleas of a young woman who was
emotionally drained and swallowed up by daily responsibilities even
though she loved being a stay-at-home mother. The following entries,
during the years before Mary and I met, prove it.

Early 1982:

But, oh, Lord, there are moments when the demands of a toddler
and being pregnant are just too much for me. I can't stop crying!
I feel like a failure as a mother. The house is in shambles, there's
laundry reaching to the ceiling, and a bare refrigerator.

Summer and Fall 1982:

Oh, Lord, sometimes I feel so inadequate as a mother . . . and yet
I feel like I never get any real time to myself. I need more gifts
like Jim gave me for our anniversary . . . two free hours with no
responsibility of kids. I didn't know what to do but then chose to
go to the public library to write letters.

March 1985, mothering a five-year-old, a three-year-old, and a ten-month-old:

I wonder at my parenting. I am afraid of the anger that erupts
and belches from me on days when I am unusually fatigued
or bogged down with a cold or sundry obligations or just feeling tied down and hemmed in. I've always professed that even
national leaders, who can command an entire nation, would be

blithering idiots at day's end after dealing with a roomful of toddlers. Yes, those little ones are so sweet and precious, but, oh, how they require constant love, attention, and guidance as they learn about life. I feel deep down that I am a good mother, but I easily get frustrated by the mundane and constant vying for my time from all of them, from Jim—and, yes, even from myself.

Sometimes I needed to look for humor in situations, or I'd end up daft. One of my children was having a rough morning, crying and whining. The poor tyke refused my attempts at comfort and consolation. Knowing that someday I might wonder how I kept my cool, I hurriedly wrote down everything that caused the distress. Please note: this all occurred within mere minutes.

My child couldn't get underwear on, couldn't get Cheerios on the spoon, the blanket wasn't tucked in right, the fork fell into the syrup, the shirt wasn't fitting right, the syrup "wasn't right" (whatever that meant), couldn't get vitamins out of the jar, got angry when I helped count them, and couldn't find a moon-shaped vitamin.

Fast forward almost twenty-five years when this child earned a PhD in analytical chemistry. Ah, doesn't the need for precision in the episode above make perfect sense now?

Mother-to-mother support was desperately needed, and I couldn't rely totally on nearby families to supply it all. Praying to find that assistance within my own community, I thankfully discovered the St. Thomas More Playgroup, created in October 1981 and based from the St. Thomas More Catholic Church in Iowa City.

Looking back at the first gathering I attended in February 1982, I chuckle. Driving to the church, I was nervous. How many women and children would be there? Would the women there like me? Would this provide the support I sought? Imagining a large, established group, I was surprised to find only three mothers, including myself, and a handful of children. Welcomed immediately, I knew I'd come home. This was it, my group, a comfortable fit for my children and me. Playgroup gradually grew, and within a few years, it exploded in numbers.

For nine and a half years, I coordinated playgroup, joined by a competent team of fun, hardworking women who divvied up the jobs and held meetings to discuss the ins and outs of running a group that flourished to over sixty families by the end of my tenure. Members participated in a wide variety of activities that included the weekly Friday morning playgroup, moms' night out, couples' night out, a weekly Bible study, meals to moms after a baby was born, a babysitting co-op, newsletters, a phone tree for urgent prayer requests, and many other meaningful ministries.

I can't begin to imagine what kind of mother I'd have been without this playgroup's astounding support. I could always count on multiple ideas for parenting challenges since viewpoints were as varied as the group's members, who hailed from all over the United States and from a few foreign countries as well.

Who kept me grounded during this time period? Jim, of course. Playgroup. Jim's family. My family. And frequent letters back and forth from my friend Gloria, who had two young boys. They all reaffirmed that good parenting is time consuming with many rewards inherent in each day.

Summer 1986:

Life has settled here lately. Perhaps it's because the kids are at ages that are a little more manageable and easier to relate to. Jill is now six; Elizabeth, four; and Jonathan, two. I can actually get beds made in the morning now. I can get two to three loads of dishes washed per day instead of the days it took for just one load last year. I can now get some entire magazines read during my spare time instead of reading only bits and pieces last year. I can finally get folded clothes put away within two to three days rather than the usual one-week period last year.

This entry takes me to the time Mary and I met. When she joined playgroup, her experience actually became the impetus for a new rule. When Mary gave birth to Michael, she was entitled to the "Meals for Moms." Various members signed up to prepare at least eight to ten days' worth of dinners. This benefit provided not only warm, nutritious food but also a chance to show off the newborn.

When her meals drew to a close, I walked over for a visit. "So, what kinds of food did people bring?" I saw her slight hesitation. "What?"

"Well, we got some lasagna."

"Yum. I love lasagna. What else?" Oh, but I was nosy.

"That was pretty much it except for one meatloaf with a big onion in the middle."

"What do you mean?"

"We got eight lasagnas. Actually, eight in a row." Seeing my shock, she added, "But they were all different. And good. Really good. We loved every one of them."

Then we started to laugh. Eight lasagnas in a row? No one could've dreamed up that scenario. Rest assured, that never happened to another playgroup mom again. From that point on, when a member took a meal, she had to list what she planned to make.

Later journal entries showed mothering was less intense as my children grew, reflecting that freedom by showing a less-stressed mother. More joys of parenting were chronicled, and a woman with better rest, more confidence in her mothering, and more free time emerged. Me time was still a precious commodity, don't get me wrong, but it was easier to fit in than before. Looking back, I only wish I could've given that worn-out mother with the young children in the early 1980s even a smidge of the bountiful time I have now. That young mother would've devoured it. I know this because I remember her well.

June 1987, mothering a seven-year-old, a five-year-old, and a three-year-old:

What is it about mother pride that allows one to be so proud of one's child?! Tonight Elizabeth and Jill had their dance recitals. It was Elizabeth's first one, Jill's third. Even though some of the time they were obviously out of step, forgetting parts, and appearing lost (esp. Elizabeth), I was so proud of them that I could burst, and I was smiling from ear to ear. Yes, mother pride overlooks those obvious technical flaws and instead feels their self-confidence, trying, and being the best they can be. Mother pride is truly unconditional love at its finest.

June 1987:

Jonathan made a structure out of Legos. He was so proud of it, and I encouraged this self-satisfaction by remarking on how long it took and how proud he must feel. It was also time we were heading for bed. He didn't want to go to bed because he wanted to take his work apart and put the pieces away. Instead, I suggested he leave it on the kitchen table, so Daddy could see it, and he excitedly agreed.

Now, after getting all three in bed and after I've soaked in a soothing bubble bath, I come out, and I see his Lego artwork very precisely placed where his chair at the table is. What a safe place . . . a perfect place . . . his place!

Mary moved away around the time I wrote those entries. While my intense years of mothering babies and toddlers drew to a close, hers continued for another twenty years or more. I moved into the busy world of chauffeuring children to activities, games, and lessons. A new stage for me, but Mary, still time-starved for me time, remained in the stage I was leaving.

Co-op Connections

Kathy Jindra

Sometimes I ask myself: how did we do it without the Internet? How did we get places without MapQuest? How did we do research on preschools, doctors, stores, vacations, illnesses, toys? We relied a lot on our friends—that's how.

It was 1982. I had just moved into a new neighborhood with my husband, Gary, two-and-a-half-year-old son, Justin, and six-month-old daughter, Sarah. It was exciting to upgrade from a two-bedroom apartment into this beautiful three-bedroom house with a yard. The only problem? I knew no one.

One morning, the doorbell rang. There stood a smiling lady with two children. She told me about a babysitting co-op and asked if I would like to come to their next meeting. Little did either of us know that my doorbell ringing would be the beginning of many new friendships, and that thirty-two years later, the babysitting co-op would still be going strong.

I attended that first gathering and was given my forty now-obsolete computer punch cards. That was the group's form of money. Each card was worth half an hour of babysitting. We took turns hosting evening meetings for the mothers as a way to get acquainted, so we could feel comfortable leaving our children with each other. But they turned into so much more.

My husband, Gary, knew he had to be home on time on the co-op evenings, because he was in charge of the kids. I looked forward to those

meetings when we would sit, laughing and talking. Before we knew it, it
would be midnight (and some nights, 1:00 a.m.). When it was my turn, I
learned to host it in the family room instead of the living room, which was
at the bottom of the stairs leading up to the bedrooms. It's amazing how
loud ten to fifteen women were once they all started laughing.

Our husbands wondered what we could possibly talk about until midnight. Since it would be a month between meetings, there were all kinds
of things to catch up on. We shared suggestions and ideas about potty
training, how to get rid of the pacifier, good preschools, park district
classes, ballet teachers, and teenage babysitters (although if you found a
good one, it was really, really hard to give out her name for fear she would
then always be busy). We set up playgroups and carpools. We talked
about family trips to Disney World. We discussed the kids riding the bus
to school, the good and bad teachers they shared, when our kids would
be old enough to walk or ride their bikes to the junior high, taking our
fifteen-year-olds out driving once they earned their driver's permit, the
safety of Accutane acne medicine, sports, curfews, dating, prom, college
choices, and much, much more.

And, yes, there was even some talk about husbands, but we can't ever
let them know. It was such a good place to vent and discover there probably isn't a perfect husband out there. Like us, they all have their little
quirks, but we are blessed to have them.

Each month, we paid two dollars in dues into a kitty to be used to
send flowers when a new baby was born. I had my third child, Bethany,
two years after joining, and received one of those bouquets at the hospital.
There were many babies born, which gave us even more to talk about.

Now we are all in our fifties and sixties. Fifteen years ago, we looked
at each other, laughing, realizing we hadn't used each other to watch our
kids in years. We can't give up our monthly meetings, but it seems silly
to keep calling ourselves "the babysitting co-op." So we are now just "the
co-op." Friends have moved, but there are still ten women in our group.
One dear friend passed away, but her memory will always be with us. We

no longer spend our kitty to send flowers for new babies, but for our own surgeries and illnesses.

It took our husbands years to finally realize there were no kids to watch when we had our gatherings. Now, on the evenings we meet, they go out to dinner together. At least twice a year, we combine our groups and let them take us out. Our conversations have turned to our parents' health and nursing homes, our health and surgeries (cancer, knee replacements, heart attacks, and pacemakers, to name a few), vacations, retirement, our children's weddings, and most fun of all: our grandchildren.

Moving to this neighborhood thirty-two years ago and having that doorbell ring was such a blessing. The friendships I have gained from the co-op fill me with happiness. And you just can't find that from the Internet.

Kathy Jindra lives in Westmont, Illinois, with her husband, Gary. They have three children and five granddaughters. Kathy works at her family business but in her spare moments will be found enjoying time with friends and family (especially her granddaughters). Kathy's life has truly been blessed with wonderful friends and a loving family.

CHAPTER FIVE

The Write Stuff

Dear Mary, how did you combine
motherhood and writing?

Mary Potter Kenyon

"Are you working on one of your little stories?"

The question was a veiled insult, meant to belittle my writing. I wrote only nonfiction, so they weren't even "stories," and there was nothing "little" about what I was trying to accomplish as a writer. I'd begun writing in 1988 when I was pregnant with my fourth child. While it may have begun as a hobby, my dream was to make a career of it someday. When I'd dropped out of graduate school to concentrate on caring for my growing brood, I searched for a way to make extra income from home. I had always loved writing, so it seemed a natural fit.

My first published piece had been a cinch to pen. I wrote an essay about the practice of praying over our children every night. Dan, Beth, and little Michael seemed to sleep better after we'd begun the ritual, so we'd continued, praying out loud and asking for God's protection and guidance. They'd join in, asking God to help them be good the next day. Rachel was a newborn when that essay appeared in the now-defunct *Praying* magazine. I have it, along with the fifty-dollar check stub, framed and hanging near my desk to this day, a visual reminder of my humble beginnings into the world of freelance writing and publishing. While I found the physical act of writing came with ease, it was the fifty-dollar check in the mail that clinched it. I decided right then that I was going to be a writer.

If I'd known then what I know now about the profession, would I have continued? If I'd known what it is like to get three rejections in a single week? The cringe-worthy moments upon spotting typos in a published work? Signing with a publisher, only to pull out of a contract mere weeks before a book release because I couldn't trust them? To net not just one agent but an unprecedented three, only to be disappointed with their work? Or worse, getting fired by one? If I could have foreseen the pain of repeated rejection and the frustration inherent in pursuing publication, would I have continued writing?

In a word, yes. It was a way to funnel my creative energy, to test my stubborn tendencies, and to follow the dream I'd held since I was a child: becoming an author. And the bottom line was that, despite how little money it brought, writing was a way to make extra income from home.

And there was always a pressing need to add to our family income. I'd already become adept at couponing, saving thousands at the grocery store. Refunding (now called "rebating") netted an additional $100 a month from plentiful manufacturer refunds. So fifty dollars in one fell swoop for a couple hours of writing seemed the ideal "hobby" for a stay-at-home mom.

In the next twenty years, I would net hundreds of published clips in the form of articles for magazines and newspapers along with more than a dozen essays in anthologies. The holy grail for writers everywhere, the first published book, came in 1996, with the release of *Home Schooling from Scratch*, a thin tome I wrote after my fifth child was born when my husband was temporarily unemployed and could care for our children.

Up until that $500 advance check from the publisher, David hadn't taken my writing very seriously. In fact, I'd felt like I had to fight for any writing time. I carried a notebook everywhere I went. If a child fell asleep in the back seat while I was driving, I'd pull over to the curb and frantically write before he or she woke up. I scribbled away on a legal pad as I sat on the toilet lid while toddlers bathed. I made notes on the back of grocery lists in the store. I eagerly welcomed my children's desire to have me sit near them as they fell asleep, because I could write by the dim bulb of a nightlight. When I teach beginning writing workshops now, I bring along a laminated 8 x 10 photo from that era. There I am in 1994, pecking away at a typewriter with baby Matthew in a backpack, peeking over my shoulder. This was my reality, the "glamorous life of a writer," I tell those young mothers in my classes who lament their lack of writing time.

I was by no means a prolific writer. I'd send out an article or two each month, less during the months after a baby was born. Checks were few and far between in those early years, and I occasionally wrote just for a subscription to a favorite magazine or newsletter. For a long time, however, money was the only way to legitimize my writing in my husband's estimation. When I won third place in a poetry contest, his "How much did you win?" said it all. If there wasn't payment, then I hadn't accomplished anything. Yes, that "Are you working on one of your little stories?" had come from the mouth of the husband who would later become one of my biggest supporters. It's a wonder I continued writing when there was so little encouragement from the home front. But I'd managed to discover a creative outlet in a world of sippy cups and diapers, and I had at least one person who understood, even when my husband didn't. I had Mary, who was also a writer. She encouraged me, commiserated with me, and at some point, began critiquing my work. It was her Lenten resolution that once prompted me to submit one piece a week instead of my usual one a month. From Ash Wednesday through Easter, I strived to meet Mary's submission rate.

Mary was the first one I turned to in my early writing career. David would eventually usurp that position, becoming the major supporter of my endeavors, with Mary a close second in that department. Yes, my husband did eventually redeem himself, signing on as president of the Team Mary Fan Club around the same time my first book was published in 1996. No one would ever guess there had been a time when David had simply tolerated his wife's "little hobby." By then, he was encouraging my lone writing sessions at restaurants and bragging me up to friends and relatives. I could turn to David and Mary whenever I got a rejection. And there were plenty of those.

By 2012, my husband had also become first reader for much of my work. For a nonwriter, he was adept at coming up with a better word and spotting errors. He was also extremely understanding of those times I went inside my head while working on a project. In fact, we were so close by then that I sometimes felt like he wanted to crawl up in there with me. It was David who encouraged me to write about our marriage and the difference his cancer experience had made in our relationship. David was the one who'd had the idea I should write a book about the history of couponing. He never lived to see either published, dying unexpectedly of a heart attack in March 2012. I didn't miss a single week writing my couponing newspaper column because, ironically, David had given me ideas for two weeks' worth of columns the day before he died.

Seven months after my husband's death, I signed a book contract for *Coupon Crazy*, the book he had encouraged me to write. A few months later, I signed another for *Chemo-Therapist*, the book on caregiving he'd inspired, from a manuscript he'd read and approved. It had needed a major overhaul because I'd grown as a writer in the five years since I'd completed it. Shortly after that, I signed a contract for *Refined By Fire*, a book that wouldn't have existed if it weren't for the loss of him.

David didn't live to see any of this, but Mary was there for all of it: the submission process, the waiting, the editing and revising, and the subsequent marketing efforts. Mary saw all that preceded these book contracts: a book acceptance that soured, my firing one agent and being fired by another, and the hours I'd put into my writing in recent years. Mary was at my side when all that hard work was rewarded with three of my books being released in the space of fifteen months—a writer's dream.

And it was Mary who knew the truth about my writing success: I would have given it all up to have just one more day with the man who was the wind beneath my wings, my husband, David.

Mary Jedlicka Humston

"Oh, Mary, I just got another rejection."

"What? You got an agent? Wow, that's great."

"I really thought that poem would be accepted."

"Guess what? My little haiku won first place. First place."

"How many rejections can a person take? Geesh."

"My article was the cover story. Can you believe it?"

"This rejection really hurt. I have to admit I cried when I opened the email and saw the routine form letter."

Was it a fluke or just pure luck that Mary and I loved to write? Did this shared interest cement our friendship even more? We may never know. What I do know is we have helped each other become better writers than we were before we met.

I don't recall when we began sharing our work, but once we started, rough drafts of poetry, fiction, and essays often accompanied our letters. We critiqued each other's pieces, developing our own language of editing marks, arrows, and scribbles. We eked out comments on organization and grammar, sometimes just circling a paragraph with a big question mark. No offense was taken. If it had, we'd have quit being each other's extra pair of eyes long ago. In the end, all those pieces shared back and forth in the mail, and later in emails, led us to this project: our book.

But where did my interest in writing begin?

A carpeted step near the top of Grandma Loretta and Grandpa John's curving stairway in their almost-century-old farmhouse was the setting for my first memory of creating a poem. I sat alone (that in itself was a rarity in a large family) with paper and pencil and scribbled away. My age or what the poem was about, I don't recall, but I remember feeling proud. Looking back, I wonder if my love of writing might've begun then.

It's amazing how something in my head can be translated onto paper and how with further concentration words can even rhyme. Milli, a member of a writer's group I attend, frequently reminds us we're working with just twenty-six letters. That's it. And yet, look at what comes from them. The joy of creating with those nominal letters, beginning with a young girl's excited poetry effort, showed me what writing could be like. I'd have to say I've been a writer ever since—and a reader too. For me, the two go hand in hand.

I discovered *Stuart Little* and *Nancy Drew* on the shelves of the small bookcase tucked away in the back corner at my country school. Nancy's adventures consumed me. As a young girl, I decided to write my own mystery series in the same vein as *Nancy Drew*. My main character was— get this—Ellen Draw. Obviously, that idea didn't progress far.

In high school, I registered for as many English classes as possible and joined the newspaper and yearbook staffs.

Then came time for college. Most career options for young women in 1972 centered on teaching, nursing, or being a secretary. Few females deviated from those paths. Heading to the skies and leading a glamorous life as a stewardess sounded fun, but my guidance counselor brought me down to earth. I didn't have the appropriate qualifications. Having good grades and numerous extracurricular activities, I was stymied by the response. The reason? Very simple. I didn't meet the height requirement. My almost-five-foot-two stature wasn't tall enough. Disappointed because there was nothing I could do about being short, I rallied my spirits and decided to become a teacher. My major was English.

My teaching career began at Bellevue, a small Iowa community along the Mississippi River. The summer before my fourth year, I became pregnant and decided to journal about this experience with the vague notion of possibly sending portions to a mothering magazine. I handed my rough draft to a friend, a recently new mom, for her comments. She honestly but kindly said she couldn't relate to my entries, explaining her pregnancy had been so different from mine. Here came a new reality in my early writing life. Instead of recognizing hers as just one opinion and not what everyone else might think, I silently accepted her feedback without question and put the manuscript away. My shoulders weren't muscled enough to bear critiques. A few months later, a popular parenting magazine published diary entries from a pregnant woman. Talk about disappointment. I'd had the idea but hadn't followed through. Today that manuscript still sits tucked away somewhere.

Three young children later, as a full-time mom at home, I wrote just enough articles and poems to compile some acceptances, along with many rejections. I was fortunate to have my faithful letter-writing friend, Mary. Writing her kept my skills in shape and later provided a great source of encouragement and support. Somehow Mary wrote despite how many children she had or how many times she and David moved. Her writing continued to be published. Many articles. Essays. A book about homeschooling on a budget. Mary inspired me then and continues to do so now.

Support and feedback from writing groups also helped. Two groups currently guide my endeavors, as did two others I attended years ago. Inspiration emanates from classes, whether about poetry or learning how to navigate the publishing world. At one how-to-get-published course sponsored by a local community college in a town thirty miles away, a new friendship developed. Nora and I, both from Iowa City, carpooled that one-hour round-trip, and our relationship flourished. Eventually, we developed a weekly sharing of writing suggestions, ideas, and critiques as well as enjoying hot tea, goodies, and lively conversations. Despite busy lives, trips, illness, or unexpected circumstances, we continue this tradition, rarely missing a week.

I recently learned the advantages of attending conferences and workshops. They provide incentive, inspiration, and the opportunity to meet other writers from around the country.

So, how do I write? What's my routine? I'd love to say I'm very organized and have everything filed in its proper place, easily accessible at a moment's notice. However, I have ideas scribbled on notepad slips, the backs of envelopes, and scratch paper and printed off the computer. I don't have an office or a private desk, just a computer desk in the front room. Because of that, papers are cluttered into organized (to me, that is) piles by the computer, on the counter by our landline telephone, and in drawers. Some are even in the laundry room. Sharp No. 2 pencils and old scrap paper for my rough drafts are my go-to pieces of equipment. Composing on the computer occasionally happens, but typically it's the pencil and paper that get my brain clicking and ticking.

It would be ideal to write three hours every single day and send out pieces every week. In reality, though, I write when I can, depending on what Jim and I are doing, how I'm feeling, or what other volunteer, church, or club-related obligations are on the schedule. Pieces are mailed out usually after inordinate editing and often with a deadline as the impetus.

I wish I was never plagued by frustration, nervousness, or discouragement. However, I get frustrated when ideas stall or wither, or I'm too tired, busy, or brain-weary to sit and write. I also get nervous, sometimes to the point of anxiety, wondering if I'll be creative enough and whether my work will be accepted. And, yes, I get discouraged when it's rejected or when an opportunity was missed because an idea didn't flow by the deadline. Plus, if we had to depend on my writing as part of our family income, we'd be sunk. Thank heaven, Jim supports my writing, in more ways than one.

I'd like to say I know everything there is to know about the art of good writing, but no one reading this book would believe that. A writer is always learning. Always.

Still, I write, usually while sipping hot tea. My emotions yo-yo with feelings of competency and self-confidence to the complete opposite, wondering how in the world I ever thought I could be a writer and seriously doubting whether I have any ability at all.

Sometimes it'd be easier on my nerves if I didn't write. It would free up time. Greater financial rewards would result if I did something else, but I don't write for the money or the fame. I write because I need to. Have to. Want to. Love to.

And that is something my dear friend Mary completely understands.

The Quodlibet Quartet

Nora L. Steinbrech

Quodlibet: an exercise in philosophical or theological discussion.

The Q2 is a bridge group composed of four retired educators who have been meeting monthly for close to forty years. We are a diverse group with not a lot in common, save the twelve times we gather each year for cards and serendipitous conversations.

It was 1977, and I was in my second year as an elementary school principal. This was back in the days when these positions were scarce, and an administrator wearing a skirt and high heels was indeed a rare species.

I take credit for organizing the Quodlibet Quartet. My grandparents and father taught my brother and me how to play bridge when we were in high school; I continued to enjoy bridge during my college years. Unfortunately, a husband, teaching job, and graduate school left little leisure time. I did miss playing, so when the master's degree had been earned and textbooks retired, it seemed a good time to return to the game. Without much difficulty, I found three acquaintances who readily agreed to become charter members.

Deborah was a close friend and colleague through many of my teaching years. We shared confidences, losses, triumphs, and a feverish interest in medieval royalty. Hers was a home with a turret and stained glass windows. Spider webs are encouraged and embellished in her cavernous great room. She informed us that she bears a likeness to Queen Elizabeth II, to which we other three responded with polite smiles and nods. She has been a steady support to her husband, who has endured many operations that have staved off repeated cancer attacks. She plays in many bridge groups, pens professional-level calligraphy, and has never had her ears pierced. Deborah is the only one of us who has a child, a quirky, carefree woman nearing fifty years of age. We have listened to many accounts of her daughter's victories and missteps, her loves and heartaches from elementary school through college and beyond. At times, we have not regretted our childless state, but at others we have envied the close tie between Deborah and her daughter.

Then there is Trudy, who got the job I would like to have had. After we were at work in our respective schools, we occasionally bumped into one another at administrator meetings. Being the only two females in the group, it was natural to get acquainted. Trudy is a traveler and risk-taker. She has stepped foot on all seven continents, been the president of a nationally recognized organization, and broken her shoulder skiing in Colorado. Her home is adorned with pictures and artifacts from her many adventures.

Kathy was the original fourth member. I taught her son in fifth grade. When he heard that I loved to play tennis, he assured me his mother was a really, really good player. Consequently, she and I became good friends and tennis partners. Happy, easygoing, with a great sense of humor, she viewed life a little differently. Her husband is a mechanical engineer, and she spent her days looking after her three children and her lakeside home. They vacationed in Hawaii, Colorado, Minnesota, and St. Croix, but when she was with the bridge group, she listened to our grumblings and school talk and good-naturedly laughed or sympathized, whichever was needed.

After a few years in the group, Kathy moved to Florida and was replaced by Bernadette. Berni's spiked hair is red . . . sometimes fuchsia, depending on the mood of her insane hairdresser. She sports a huge, perennial smile and a strong, sturdy figure ideal for displaying her outrageous outfits and sparkly jewelry. She was beginning to settle into a future of spinsterhood when, in her fifty-second year, she met a perfectly lovely fellow. The Q2 enjoyed the vicarious thrills of the courtship, engagement, and finally the beautiful wedding where the happy couple jumped over the broomstick to begin their married life. Our wedding gift to them was crystal wine glasses and an extremely expensive bottle of wine, which they recently enjoyed on their fifth anniversary.

Through thirty-eight years, we have watched each other grow older, lose parents, change jobs and hair color, abandon old ideas, and acquire new interests. At about the fifth year of our club's existence, I suggested we take turns keeping a record of our meetings, documenting important events and the life experiences we share over the bridge table. We are now filling our fourth journal. The following is an excerpt from journal number three:

July 2011

Bridge was at Deborah's on a warm and sunny Wednesday. We noticed the dragonfly copper sculpture we had given her in memory of her mother. She had placed it just outside her front door under a weeping cherry tree. It is apparent that Deborah has an artist's eye.

Of course, we sat down to chat before bridge, and, unexpectedly, Nora surprised each of us with a lovely little book that opened to reveal a treat of homemade cookies and a brightly wrapped truffle. Included was a note thanking us for helping her with the Green Thumb Project city tour of her garden. We also heard several entertaining stories from Berni about their visit to her father-in-law's home in Texas. Berni is kindhearted and genuinely fond of the old gentleman.

Bridge play was stimulating but somewhat strange. We had one round where neither side had a game and in four hands, only ninety points were scored below the line!

High score was Deborah, but she declared that all the winnings should go to Trudy in honor of her birthday the following day. She then announced that she had a sweet dessert . . . surprise! It was a delicious red velvet birthday cake, served on her mother's beautiful china. The china prompted an interesting discussion about its possible value and warnings from us about not putting it in the dishwasher.

Since Nora will be back at work (!), our next game will be at Trudy's on August 24th at 7 p.m.

Addendum: By 5 p.m. that afternoon, Deborah reported via email that after checking suggested sources, she found her mother's china set is worth at least $1800! She's not going to put it in the dishwasher!

What is the adhesive that binds a group of women with different backgrounds, personalities, and interests? It isn't the quality of card playing. Perhaps it is a sense of caring and, quite frankly, the entertaining stories and accounts of adventures that keep us coming back month after month. Over these many years of the Q2's existence, no one has missed more than one, perhaps two, of the more than 456 bridge games. Over the years, we have celebrated birthdays, weddings, anniversaries, and a variety of successes. We have been there for one another as parents have passed away and other hardships have been endured.

Maybe it's a sense of continuity. I think coming together each month provides a respite from the personal trials, illnesses, disappointments, and concerns we humans inevitably must face, as well as societal upheavals that we struggle to understand. The group is there with sympathy, points of view which often differ, support, and, thank goodness, a sense of humor that is often exactly what is needed.

Who would have thought when we dealt the cards the first time, the Q2 would still be active and energetic these thirty-eight years later?

Most assuredly, we are a *longest and strongest suit.*

Nora Steinbrech lives in Iowa City, Iowa. She has a PhD from the University of Iowa. Nora retired from an administrative position in the Iowa City Community School District and is currently a Practicum Supervisor in the College of Education at the University of Iowa. She is married to William, who has no interest in playing bridge but does enjoy the stories she brings home from the bridge table conversations. She is a zealous gardener, ferocious tennis competitor, enthusiastic amateur writer and painter, and underachieving bridge player.

CHAPTER SIX

In Sickness and in Health

Dear Mary, have you ever experienced ill
health? How did that affect your friendships?

Mary Potter Kenyon

"I felt so sick this afternoon, with an upset stomach and nausea. I was so shaky and hot, I thought I was going to die," said Elizabeth over the phone. My daughter was relating an all-too-familiar scenario.

"Did you get so hot you wanted to take off all your clothes?" I asked, and we both laughed a little.

"And were you so tired after the episode that you wanted to just crawl in bed and fall asleep?"

"Yes, I actually did lie down." I heard her surprise. "How did you know?"

"I lived with that when I had chronic fatigue syndrome. It was the worst symptom, one I experienced almost every day, and some nights too."

"Every day? How could you stand it?"

How could I stand it, indeed?

I was a relatively healthy mother of four children in 1990. I walked daily with my youngest two, pushing Michael in a stroller, carrying Rachel strapped in a backpack. When I became violently ill the day after Thanksgiving, I was certain I'd gotten food poisoning. Besides spending half the morning in the bathroom, I was overcome with an extreme fatigue. My children had to entertain themselves that day. And the next. And the next.

While the initial stomach upset and nausea improved slightly, the fatigue did not. Extreme fatigue was accompanied by frequent, intense headaches, joint pain, muscle aches, and those bouts of irritable bowel syndrome (IBS) that began to rule my life. Suddenly, the mother who walked a mile with ease didn't have the energy to walk down the block. My children got accustomed to a mom who spent most of her mornings in the bathroom. My husband did what he could, settling the children with bowls of cereal in front of the television every morning before he went to work, and calling at noon to see how I was doing. Dan, who was eleven, would stay home from school to help on my worst days. David put the kids to bed every night, because I'd collapse in exhaustion before then. Even when I went to sleep at 8:00 p.m., I'd wake up twelve hours later exhausted. It was a fatigue that sleep and rest never lifted.

Thus began an odyssey of visits to doctors and unanswered questions, which eventually led to visits to specialists and more unanswered questions. At some point, as test after test came back negative, my primary doctor began looking at me differently. The day he snapped, "Why do you have to know what is wrong with you?" is the same day I ended up in an emergency room with a full-blown anxiety attack. I thought I must be dying.

"Give her a shot," the doctor on call barked to the nurse after hearing my saga. Then he pulled my husband aside. "Quit coddling her. There's nothing wrong with her," I heard him say.

As blessed, calming medication coursed through my veins, hot tears ran down my cheeks. The nurse took my hand and leaned in close. "Don't listen to him. You know you are sick. You know something's wrong. Don't give up. You'll find out what is wrong."

The fact that Mary, ninety miles away, had also been experiencing a mystery illness for months boggles my mind now. Immune system disorders, chronic fatigue, and fibromyalgia are familiar terms today. Back then, though, this was something new and unusual. Thousands of women and men suffered in silence, being misdiagnosed, mistreated, and misunderstood. I was writing to two women who'd responded to a pen pal ad where I mentioned my illness. Both had been diagnosed with chronic fatigue syndrome (CFS) with symptoms nearly identical to my own.

After nearly a year of searching for answers and with a stack of medical journal articles and a twenty-page letter from one of the women with CFS, I visited my mother's doctor. The only helpful diagnostic test used then was one for Epstein-Barr. Blood tests revealed that my Epstein-Barr reading was elevated, and I got my diagnosis. That, and the medication the doctor prescribed for the IBS, gave me back my life.

I don't remember much about our letter writing during this time. Did Mary and I write less frequently? More frequently about our mutual miseries? I did a lot of sedentary activities then: refunding and couponing at my desk, writing, watching television with the kids, napping. Perhaps I wrote Mary quite often. Like Mary, I learned that one day of physical activity could mean three days of recuperation, so I didn't do much outside the house unless I knew I could rest for a day or two. I lost thirty-five pounds, netting comments about how great I looked. I resented this because I felt so awful. I might not have looked ill, but I sure felt it.

I'll never forget the day Mary visited me to participate in a video taping of a planned coupon shopping trip. As the New York crew set up their equipment, Mary leaned over and whispered, "They'll never know they're filming two ill women." She was right. We rallied for the cameras, clipping coupons and making small talk for two hours, then strategically shopping in front of the team for three more. No one would guess from looking at us that we were fighting an invisible enemy. No one but our families would know we spent most of the next two days on our respective couches, either.

After eighteen months of this, I'd read enough about CFS to know that some women had found relief through a pregnancy. Sure enough, during the second trimester of my fifth pregnancy in 1993, the fatigue lifted. I was my former self. Only the IBS remained, but I had medication that helped with that. It would continue to plague me for much of my life, peaking during future pregnancies. I worked part-time at a library in 2003 when I was pregnant with my eighth. When I realized there were days I was spending more time in the bathroom than at the desk, I quit the best job I'd ever had. Whether menopause or gallbladder removal brought relief, I'll never know, but bouts of IBS are few and far between now.

I can't say if I was a good friend to Mary or not during this period when she continued to struggle with fatigue. The pregnancy that cut short my CFS ended in an emergency C-section, where I lost so much blood I had to have several transfusions. I remember Mary telling me she didn't recognize my handwriting from the letter I wrote her while in the hospital. I came home weak and exhausted. My husband lost his job a week later.

It was during this period of upheaval that I wrote my first book. What others might have viewed as my incredible energy could have been sheer desperation. By the time Emily was born three years later, I was helping my husband with our used bookstore, running a home business, and seeing some success with my writing.

Was it around this time that Mary and I made the mutual decision to throw out all our old letters? Neither one of us remembers. In fact, there's a lot I don't remember from those busy years. Why didn't we send the letters back to each other? I'd like to see them, like to know that I commiserated with Mary's continual struggle with her health. I know I breathed a sigh of relief when she got a diagnosis and the right medication finally helped her.

The next big health crisis in our life was when David was diagnosed with oral cancer in 2006. Mary's thyroid cancer followed too closely for my comfort. Her phone call came in late December 2007, during a particularly hard winter and after David and I had made an offer on a house in town.

I remember hanging up the phone and just sitting there numb. I couldn't bear that Mary might have to go through all that David had endured. I cried a little. What could I possibly do to help?

I could write her. I probably sat down and wrote her right then. Was this the first time I would write "I love you" to Mary? I'd often signed my letters "With love," or "Love," but it was still difficult to write or say "I

love you" to anyone but my mother, husband, and children. Or did the
first "I love you" come after David's death? Those words came easily for
David after his cancer, but in 2008 they still didn't for me.

Unlike my husband's fifty-fifty odds, Mary's prognosis was good. She
underwent surgery, a radioactive iodine treatment, and radiation. I wrote
her more frequently then, and I sent her cards and a flat-rate priority
mailer of the high-protein foods that David had enjoyed. I shopped at my
sister's consignment store for the softest V-neck shirts I could find. What
I didn't do was what I most wanted to: go and be with Mary.

I will always regret not visiting Mary during this time. The winter
weather was terrible, we were in the middle of a move, and I had a four-
year-old and five other children at home. I wasn't going much of anywhere
at all, and I had never driven farther than the thirty miles to Dubuque by
myself. But my friend was going through something awful, and our only
personal contact through it all was that single phone call and letters.

Mary Jedlicka Humston

Who knew that the tiny textured spot by my left eye was cancer? You could barely see it. The only oddity? It would bleed occasionally after wiping my face with a washcloth while removing makeup at night. It would fester for a day or two and then heal. Hardly visible and with almost no bump, it looked normal again. Around three weeks later, the same thing happened. Bleed. Heal. Look normal. I'd read enough about skin cancer to know that after a third or fourth round of this, consulting a doctor shouldn't be delayed. Sure enough, the biopsy showed skin cancer.

It was so close to my eye that my bottom lashes almost touched it. Because of that, an appointment was scheduled at the University of Iowa Hospitals and Clinics to have a specialist extract it using the Mohs method, an outpatient procedure where a thin layer of skin is removed and tested. This is repeated as often as necessary to ensure healthy, clear margins with no tissue containing cancer.

As I write this, the first part of the Mohs procedure is being completed. The basal cell carcinoma was removed and is being tested by the laboratory. Did they get it all? Are the margins clear? Or will there need to be another excision? It could be more than an hour to get the results.

I'm sitting in a straight-back chair while my husband Jim is reading a book and sitting on the doctor's stool with its round seat and wheels. It's a quiet companionship we have here: he drinking coffee, me drinking tea, both of us set for the next round of whatever is to come. The skin around my eye that isn't covered by the bandage is starting to turn yellow, a precursor to a possible black eye when the procedure is over. That's understandable considering the cutting and stitching that area will endure today.

So, while waiting for the next step, I paw through the bag I packed with a variety of items to keep me busy. There's the current book I'm reading, a couple of magazines, and my writing materials. I dig paper and pencils out and decide to work on our book. And the chapter I settle on? How appropriate that I work on "In Sickness and in Health" while dealing with a medical issue.

Mary and I were healthy young mothers when we first met. Diseases? None. Surgeries? I'd only had a tonsillectomy when I was twenty-three years old in 1978, and then a cesarean delivery with my oldest daughter, Jill, in 1980. Serious illness? None. I wasn't aware of any for her either.

But three years after Mary moved, both of us were affected by mysterious illnesses: me in April 1990, and Mary that fall. Not much was known about chronic fatigue syndrome, fibromyalgia, and other similar illnesses back then. All we knew is we were both overcome by debilitating exhaustion. I doubt few letters were exchanged then. It was all we could do to simply function. After climbing out of bed, getting breakfast for the kids, and sending Jill and Elizabeth off to school, I'd collapse on the sofa while five-year-old Jonathan played nearby or watched children's programs. Talk about mother guilt. Having him watch so much TV frustrated me, but what else could I do? When Jim was home, they'd head off for some fun activity, and I'd return to bed just as exhausted as when I'd awakened.

After a couple of months, the illness eventually leveled off to where I functioned fairly well if I napped for two to three hours. These daily naps were crucial to my well-being. If I missed one, I faced fuzzy-headed thinking, headaches, and mind-numbing exhaustion. This was my life for eleven years. Yes, eleven years. During that time, our letters became lifelines. I might not have been able to do much, but I could start a letter, stop if necessary, and then pick it up again to commiserate over the fatigue, my feelings of loss, and the uncertainty of ever having a normal day of health again.

Volunteering took a hit. It had been an important part of my life, but there was only so much energy to go around, and most of it was designated for my family. I made herculean efforts to help out in my children's schools and extracurricular activities when I could, but I had to be careful not to overdo it. I had been so active, it was depressing not to give generously of my time as I'd been used to doing.

My mom put things into perspective when she said, "Mary, you've volunteered enough in the past to last a lifetime." Taking that to heart, I did what I could when I could, trying to be satisfied with my new normal.

Being able to help others produced feelings of goodwill as well as provided wells of opportunity to make friends. When volunteering significantly diminished, it was difficult to carry potential friendships much further beyond the activity we were working on, whether it be in the classroom, at the concession stands, or decorating for music events.

It was also difficult to maintain the many friendships I already had. I learned to be judicious with every bit of my limited time and energy, gravitating toward those who truly understood my illness. I needed to surround myself with positive, uplifting people. Being around negativity weighed me down, and I certainly didn't need more of that.

I'm sure there were some who didn't understand why I wasn't my usual vivacious self. Part of the problem was that I didn't look ill, although Mom always said she could see the fatigue in my eyes. I worked hard to maintain friendships, but it wasn't easy. I belonged to a few clubs and organizations, and I attended meetings, Bible studies, and luncheons when I could, but at best I was a peripheral member. To this day, I am grateful for family and friends who supported me then. They have no idea how much they sustained me.

Mary's letters of compassion were salve to the wounds in my soul. She lifted me when I was down. I'd do the same for her. We meant it when we said, "I know how you feel," because we really did.

A new doctor, a diagnosis of myofascial pain syndrome, and a new medicine changed everything in 2001, giving me a quality of life I never dreamed possible again. The medication still works and has allowed me to have some amazing experiences and accomplishments. If the symptoms should worsen in the future and return me to that life of fatigue again, I have no regrets. I have taken risks, made new friendships, and lived a life of exciting ventures and activities.

Since I still deal with this chronic illness, I am prone to light-headedness, headaches, dizziness, and neck and back pain. I might not get sick as often, but when I do, it hits hard. Traveling and illness tire me out, so I have to remind myself I'm not cured. It's not always easy, but it is significantly more manageable than it was those eleven years.

Now, as I sit here awaiting the results of the Mohs surgery, I reflect back on 2008 when I had stage three thyroid cancer surgeries and treatments. Once again, I didn't get as many letters off to Mary as I'd have liked, but when I did, it made life "normal." And Mary knew I could use more correspondence during this time, because I had done the same for her when she became her husband's caregiver after his diagnosis in 2006. We didn't just write about David's cancer. Yes, Mary sent updates to help process her feelings, but it was also crucial we detail the ordinary, everyday aspects of life. Our world wasn't just illness, and it was imperative we be reminded of that.

With my cancer coming so quickly on the heels of David's, Mary was aware of the terminology, procedures, side effects, and lengthy recovery. Along with her letters, I was fortunate to also have been surrounded by the prayers and support of many family members and friends. I don't know how I'd have handled it without their many ways of making me feel cared for. Meals, cards that arrived almost daily, flowers, visits, and telephone calls boosted my spirits. And if I didn't feel up to visiting or talking on the phone, I still appreciated those efforts because they offered Jim the opportunity to share his thoughts and pass time while I convalesced.

In the course of Mary's and my friendship, we continue to write our way through our own major and minor injuries and illnesses as well as those of our families and friends. When I complain about a malady, I write knowing she won't shake her head and sigh, "Oh, no. Not again. She's such a wimp." She knows I'm not a whiner, but that I need to get the frustration and the "I'm sick and tired of being sick and tired" mantra out of my meditation loop. I'm a pretty optimistic person, and Mary knows this, but she also knows the value of venting.

She will understand and empathize. She'll care what happens as I go through this Mohs procedure today and how discouraging it feels to have my one and only spot removed end up being skin cancer. She'll know I'm not complaining per se, because we both realize this has a 99 percent successful treatment rate. But she *gets* me. She will write back and acknowledge this experience. And it will be just one of the many ways we've helped each other through health concerns. Our letters are key elements in processing, enduring, recuperating, and healing. It's a bit of normalcy amid abnormal situations.

In fact, while Jim and I still prepare to hear what the lab results are and what the next step is with the Mohs surgery, I finish this chapter. I rummage through my bag for my special pen and stationery. While Jim is here for immediate love and support, my letter to Mary chronicles the details of this experience. I start my letter to her now, because this is what we do. We write.

PS. The Mohs surgery? Only one layer was removed. And, lucky me, no black eye.

Cherry Blossom Friendships

Lori Erickson

For much of my life, I've thought my most valuable friendships were those that have lasted a long time. But through my volunteer work as a Healing Touch Practitioner, I've come to realize that some of my most important friendships are all the more meaningful because they are short lived. I've come to think of them as my cherry blossom friendships—beautiful, fleeting, and full of wonder.

Healing Touch is a form of complementary medicine that has many similarities to the ancient Christian practice of laying on of hands for healing. In my church, we offer it as a form of ministry. Most of the people we see have been diagnosed with cancer. They come to our healing room that overlooks a courtyard garden for a weekly session in the midst of their chemotherapy or radiation treatments.

It's not surprising that friendships often form in this context. What typically takes years during the course of a normal friendship can happen very quickly under these circumstances. This is especially true for those who do not receive the cure they desperately seek. Despite their valiant struggles to live, their cancer worsens and their medical treatments lose their effectiveness. Healing Touch often becomes even more important to them as they enter hospice care.

Each time this happens, I question the wisdom of doing volunteer work that stands a good chance of making me extremely sad. When I attend the funeral of someone I've worked with, I sometimes toy with the idea of finding another form of service, like walking dogs at the animal shelter or reading to schoolchildren—activities that aren't likely to end with me in a church singing "Amazing Grace" through my tears.

Then I go right back to volunteering in our healing ministries program, because these friendships have taught me more than almost any other relationship I've had.

The first person I got close to in this way was Diane, who came to see me for Healing Touch while undergoing treatment for breast cancer. We were strangers when we were introduced, but we soon became dear friends. Nearly every week, we would meet in the healing room at our church. Before we started our session together, we'd visit, first about inconsequential things, then increasingly about more personal matters.

Every time I saw her, she found positive things to focus on. No matter what bad turn her medical condition had taken, she always found something to be grateful for. At first, I thought she was perhaps putting on a brave front, but, over time, I came to see that her sense of gratitude and optimism were utterly genuine.

That optimism came, I think, both from her deep faith and from her knowledge that she was surrounded by people who loved her. I noticed that she rarely used the word "I" in relation to her medical condition. It was always, "We're going to be trying a new treatment next week," or "We're making progress on this." She knew that she wasn't going through her journey alone.

I was also struck by the way in which Diane cared for me. In a situation in which, technically, I was the one serving her, she gave as much to me as I did to her. In that room, we shared a great deal, I think in part because we had no other ties other than that hour per week. We didn't know anyone else in each other's families or social circles. We could complain, share worries, and rejoice in each other's joys knowing that what we talked about was confidential.

As Diane approached the end of her life, she asked if I would speak at her funeral. I said yes, of course, but I also worried privately over what I would say. I had only known Diane for a short portion of her life, and I had never even seen her outside the walls of the healing room.

At the same time, I felt that I did know her in all the ways that mattered. I knew firsthand her courage, her vitality, her warmth. And as I stood in the church in front of hundreds of people, I realized I knew many of them too. Because of all those conversations with Diane, I knew about her children and grandchildren and their foibles, quirks, and histories. I knew about her siblings, book group members, and old friends from college days. I didn't know their faces, but I knew what they meant to Diane.

In my eulogy, I spoke about how much I had learned from Diane, and I told them how much she loved them all. After the service, many of them introduced themselves to me at the reception. I delighted in meeting these people I'd known only through her stories. They felt like old friends to me—after all, any friend of Diane's was a friend of mine.

Today, when I work in our church's healing room, I sometimes think of a trip I took to Japan during cherry blossom season, that brief period in spring when a gauzy shroud of pink covers parks and gardens. While there, I learned that cherry blossoms are more than just flowers to the Japanese. They are an excuse to celebrate, for families and friends meet under the flowering trees to drink, eat, and socialize. Even more importantly, they are a symbol for the transitory nature of life. The delicate cherry blossom, here today and fluttering to the ground tomorrow, is a poignant symbol of how beautiful and how brief existence is.

Diane was the first of my cherry blossom friendships, but not the last. Each one reminds me of walking underneath the blooming cherry trees in Kyoto, their petals falling like snow.

Lori Erickson grew up on a farm in northeast Iowa. She has been a freelance writer for many years and is the author of books that include The Joy of Pilgrimage, Sweet Corn and Sushi, *and* Iowa: Off the

Beaten Path. *Her articles and essays have appeared in many regional and national publications. Her website, Spiritual Travels, and blog, The Holy Rover, cover topics relating to the intersection of spirituality and travel. She lives in Iowa City with her husband.*

CHAPTER SEVEN

When Jealousy Rears Its Ugly Head

Dear Mary, have you ever envied Mary?

Mary Potter Kenyon

"I took a one-hour walk this morning and then did yoga."

"I met Nora for lunch before stopping at the library to pick up some books I had on reserve."

"Today I walked three miles along the bluff and spotted six eagles."

"Headed to a movie with some friends."

"Jim and I have couples' Bible study tonight."

Of course, Mary's letters have changed in content since the late '80s. Initially, they contained the mutual musings on raising children, couponing, writing, and reading-related topics. While her family size stayed the same, mine continued growing. I'm sure the topic of child rearing must have become a bit lopsided in the letters. I could be crowing about the first steps of one of my babies or complaining about pregnancy nausea while her youngest might be deciding on a major in college. This never seemed a problem between us. Mary was with me when I discovered Abby's first tooth. I observed genuine excitement in her eyes when I triumphantly announced the milestone. I never felt like she'd left me in the mothering dust. Mary seemed to understand. To relate.

Our infrequent visits were the same. Early on, they involved our children playing together. Later, when hers were older, Mary visited without them. The first time she came alone, I felt a stab of envy at what ease there must be in traveling without children. David and I had avoided traveling for much of our marriage, both because of the inherent cost of a trip for a cash-strapped family and because there was nothing more unpleasant than a car full of cranky children.

Anytime I experienced jealousy toward Mary, I reminded myself that our friendship wasn't about keeping score. Mary never flaunted her freedom. Even if she was no longer in the thick of mothering toddlers, she still understood. I envied her genuine openness. I was not always as open and kind. I occasionally got a jab of judgment into conversations with mothers who had chosen a different parenting path. Mary seemed much less judgmental, more accepting. I imagined that she wouldn't hesitate to befriend the Queen of England or a mother in a homeless shelter, while I would have hesitated to broach a relationship with either.

Mary's letters in the last fifteen years or so have reflected a freedom I have always wondered about. And just now, at age fifty-five, I am getting a small taste of it. My youngest is eleven years old. I've been parenting for thirty-five years, and it will be at least seven more before I can experience an empty nest or know what it is like to live a life unencumbered by children. Even in arranging time to work on this book with Mary, I had to consider something she did not: the children I have at home. *Will they be okay left alone for a day?*

If there is anything I have envied in Mary's life, it has been that relative freedom she seems to have. I use the term "relative" because I am well aware of the unfairness of comparing my life to someone else's. I know, too, that Mary experienced the same mix of feelings I did when her husband's job schedule wasn't ideal for a life with three small children. I can't know what it was like to have a husband who, as a firefighter, would be absent from home for twenty-four hours at a time. I don't want to compare my life to anyone's, least of all a friend's.

Yet, on my worst days, I do go there. There, where that tiresome working vs. stay-at-home mom, rich vs. poor, large family vs. smaller, breast vs. bottle, cloth vs. disposable measuring-stick standard resides. When I meet a woman who has never needed to contribute to her family's income, the unwelcome litany begins: *You don't know what it is to always feel like you must contribute financially.* And as a widow, there is more: *You don't know what it's like to parent alone, to be the only breadwinner. I wish I didn't have to work so hard just to pay the bills.*

I continue to engage in this inner dialogue occasionally, despite my best intentions and the realization that it was my choice to become a mother. My choice to have more children. I definitely did not choose to be a widow, but it is what it is. I certainly don't begrudge anyone their spouse because of it. I remind myself that no matter what I think I know about another woman's life, I really don't know what her choices have cost her, or whether or not her life is easier or less stressful. How could that even be measured? And why should it be? Nothing is ever that simple. I know all that.

Does envy creep into even the best relationships? I was envious of David's easygoing attitude post-cancer, his ability to nap frequently without regard to what needed to get done. I envied his ease in expressing love after he'd gone through the fire of cancer. I've envied friends' and siblings' ability to travel and even the fact that they still have their spouse. I've been jealous of other authors whose books were more successful than mine, who won contests I didn't, whose work was lauded or reviewed when mine wasn't. I've envied women whose husbands' salaries allowed them financial peace of mind. And with every stab of envy has come remorse. The face of envy is not becoming on anyone.

I'm not sure exactly when I made the decision, but I believe it was after a Bible study that condemned envy as a grave sin. I knew I would always face its temptation, so I needed a plan of action to handle it. I decided to consciously allow for those feelings of envy when they arose. I let white-hot jealousy envelop me for five minutes. Before it takes hold of my heart and soul, I banish it. Doing this means that after those miserable, wretched five minutes, I am able to feel joy for the other person. And joy is so much more pleasurable than envy.

Mary Jedlicka Humston

Envy between friends isn't comfortable to talk about, much less write about publicly. But if Mary and I had read between the lines of our letters, it should've been clear that we each desired something the other had.

During those eleven years I dealt with myofascial pain syndrome, Mary's illness went into remission. While I barely sustained energy for little more than my family, hers seemed boundless to me. It wasn't Mary's energy as much as what it allowed her to do that I fancied. You see, one of the biggest accomplishments she commandeered during that time was her writing. I occasionally chugged out a few submissions, but not very many, and most returned with rejections, while Mary's submissions and acceptances were prolific.

Despite having a large family and young children, she produced multitudes of writing credits for her resume. I wasn't consumed with envy, but I felt a deep longing for what Mary had. Articles accepted in magazines. Authoring a book. Essays in *Chicken Soup for the Soul* anthologies. There was no way I could keep up with her productivity.

Once I regained my health and devoted more time to writing, I still didn't hold a candle to what she could accomplish. In the end, my yearning turned into admiration. If only our government could've bottled Mary's determination when she sought representation for a book on caregiving through cancer. She doggedly sent out over eighty queries. Yes, over eighty. When one rejection arrived in the mail, she'd send out two or three more queries. That type of grit and dedication could change world policy.

And did I mention she loves research? I envy her ability to grab a subject by its teeth and shake it all over the place until she's bled so much information from a variety of sources that there's little left she doesn't know. How does she do that? Doing research papers in high school and college tried my patience, but Mary thrives on it. I wish I did.

Believe it or not, as Mary's success as a writer and author grew, I wasn't jealous. She earned every bit of it, because she put in the time, and I didn't. Her accomplishments spanned hours of writing. Mine were more like spit in the wind compared to her full, deep well of splashing water. However, I continued to submit my work when inspired or encouraged by deadlines. Mary often critiqued it and recommended magazines, contests, and journals for submission.

Mary is successful at almost everything she does. Take her couponing and refunding, for example. We shared this hobby/lifestyle for many years, trading and exchanging deals and stories of money saved. I suppose at one time in the early days I envied Mary's status as a coupon queen, but how could I begrudge her success when she put countless hours and research into this, too? She scoured the store ads and was so adept at pairing coupons with sales that her wise accounting saved her family lots of money, especially during lean times. I always applauded her accomplishments, and I wrote many kudos in my letters after she related the latest couponing coup.

Through the years, I've sometimes struggled with finding or making time to write. In order to do so, I've naturally had to temporarily suspend some of my leadership roles, volunteer work, church activities, and social events.

What I won't give up is exercise. I must exercise for my health. If I don't, I pay for it later on in pain and stiffness. Yes, I'm aware this time could be spent writing. And, conversely, Mary often chooses writing instead of exercise. We do what works best for each of us, and, as Mary said in our first chapter, we aren't clones.

In the end, the very things I envy about Mary are the very things that make me proud of her. Her dedication to whatever she's focused on is evident in her many speaking engagements, her work as a library director, her homeschooling, writing, researching, and her determination to always do her best.

The traits we see in each other are those we both wish we had more of, and the very things we might covet are the very things we admire in the other.

They Call Us "Shwandelly"

Wanda Sanchez

When I was asked to write an essay for *Mary & Me*, I had three immediate thoughts, beginning with: *Wow. I feel so honored to be given a place in this wonderful book!* My second thought quickly followed: *Run! That sounds way too touchy-feely-mushy-smushy for me. And this is not the time for that stuff.* Which was immediately followed by my third thought, which laid the others to rest: *Yes! I would love to tell the story of my friendship with Shelly, whom I call "my angel."* People all over the globe who have heard our story understand when I describe her that way.

Of course, I also liken her to Aunt Clara on *Bewitched*: just a tad bit goofy but so sweet, funny, and endearing. My best friend.

It all began about six years ago. Beautiful spring morning aside, I was in trouble. Serious trouble. I was living in my native California, in a lovely little apartment with manicured lawns and beautiful flowerbeds. I had willfully isolated myself from coworkers, friends, and family and was impatiently waiting to die. I was on a frantic journey to find the quickest way out of this world. I had been working toward my plan for a year, and I was strangely calm—peaceful, even, as if it was all settled. I was going to punch my own ticket on a certain date and be out of here—gone from this world. Gladly. Well, at least that's what I had planned.

But God (I sometimes call Him "Jehovah Sneaky") had other plans. Little did I know I was about to begin the most intense, scary, and awesome ride of my life! Three thousand miles across the country, in Grand Rapids, Michigan, Harley-riding, award-winning author and caregiving expert Shelly Beach was experiencing some rather unsettling thoughts, chief among them a strangely urgent compulsion to call Wanda Sanchez.

Multiple attempts to banish the "call Wanda" suggestion out of her mind over the course of a couple of weeks led her to an unwanted conclusion. She clearly *must call* Wanda Sanchez. She didn't know me; she knew of me. We hadn't spoken more than ten personal words in our few weeks of working together when she was a guest on a live radio talk show that I program across the country, and she didn't know why she should call me.

Before trying to connect, Shelly set out to discover more about me. She followed me on Twitter and friended me on Facebook, but found nothing personal. I posted about my work and the news and bragged on my family and friends, but I avoided anything about myself. Except for one thing: I loved inner-city missions. She took that one bit of information, wrote an email mentioning my passion for them, attached some music to it, and sent it to me, requesting to speak by phone, to get to know me.

When I read the email, I was bothered. I was not looking for a friend. I did NOT want to be known—by anyone. I was on final countdown, too busy, and not interested. The scent of sarcasm in my reply was overwhelming even to me as I complained out loud, "Oh, yippee. She wants to get to know me." Because all I wanted to do was hide; I was not interested in having any more people in my life that I felt the need to shield from myself and my downward spiral into hell.

After trying and failing to learn anything personal, Shelly picked up the phone and called. She was greeted by a very angry, very agitated Wanda Sanchez. If persistence looked like someone, it would be Shelly Beach. She is bold and unafraid when she has her mind set on something, especially if she feels she is being nudged by God.

What happened next can only be described as supernatural . . . a miracle, really (I don't believe in coincidence). For years, the only prayer I had ever been able to pray for myself had been one simple word: HELP! Little did I know at the time that the Creator of the Universe had His eye on me and was about to answer that prayer in ways I never expected. Help had arrived, and her name was Shelly.

From that day to this, six years and one intensive trauma treatment program later, I have learned about the beauty and blessing of true friendship. Right out of the gate, Shelly jumped in with both feet, no holds barred, saying, "THIS is what friends do!" I ended up hospitalized in the early days of our friendship, and she called and spoke to the nurses on my floor to advocate on my behalf. Because she knew how terrified I would be, she flew across the country to be with me. When she arrived, she crawled into my hospital bed and held my hand. When I was able (barely), she drove me cross country, from California to Michigan, while I slumped next to her in the front seat, mostly unconscious and very ill. Over the following couple of years while I was still ill, Shelly took almost full-time care of me.

That was the single biggest lesson of friendship I have ever learned: the gift of sacrifice, of silent strength, of presence.

The stranger across the country became my teacher, and I became hers. She became my mentor, and she became my friend. Today, we do the ministry-and-friendship thing together. We consult on PTSD/trauma across the country in churches, jails, prisons, medical hospitals, adoption agencies, women's conferences, seminars, and retreats.

Together, Shelly and I have traveled tens of thousands of miles. By plane, we once ministered to flight attendants in crisis. By train, we befriended a Katrina survivor who ran out of food early on in the trip, and we were able to bless her with more. By automobile, we've provided rides and gas for women broken down and stranded on the side of the road or at gas stations.

Shelly and I have become sisters and friends who are committed to being there for each other in all seasons of life, no matter how that looks. We have spoken to thousands of women from every walk of life about the miracle of faith, hope, and friendship.

We pray for the opportunities that are ahead to show other women what real, true, rubber-meets-the-road friendship really looks like.

In December 2014, doctors found lesions wrapped around Shelly's brain stem. She immediately had a craniotomy to help doctors identify exactly what type of lesion/growth it is that has made itself at home in her brain. As I write this, Shelly is recuperating from her surgery and will be heading to Mayo Clinic for further testing and treatment. Now it's my turn to care for her. Through her gentle care for me at my very sickest, I learned how to be a caregiver. I am honored to be walking this journey with my best friend, Shelly Beach.

Wanda Sanchez is executive producer of the longest-running radio talk show in the Northern California–San Francisco market. With more than twenty years of broadcast media experience in television and radio, Wanda is the executive publicist at a public relations/media consulting/communications start-up in Grand Rapids, Michigan. She is the cofounder of PTSDPerspectives.org with Shelly Beach. She is the coauthor of Love Letters from the Edge: Meditations for Those Struggling with Brokenness, Trauma, and the Pain of Life *(Kregel Publcations) and has been published in* World Net Daily, *the* Hope in the Mourning Bible *(Zondervan Publishers), and has written numerous articles for other publications. She speaks across the nation in prisons, mental and medical health facilities, churches, and women's conferences on the topics of trauma, hope, and healing. She can be found at PTSDPerspectives.org and WandaSanchez.com.*

CHAPTER EIGHT

Who, Me? Worry?

Dear Mary, have you ever dealt
with anxiety or worry?

Mary Potter Kenyon

I don't remember where I heard the term, but the description is apt. "Monkey mind" describes it perfectly, because it feels like a monkey jumping around inside my head.

This is how it works. A routine mammogram in October 2014 becomes nonroutine when further tests are ordered. An area of concern is seen in both breasts, so an ultrasound mammogram is needed. While the nurse informs me of this development over the phone, the monkey mind begins. *An area of concern? Both breasts?* By the time I hang up the phone, I'm certain I've got cancer. Even though I can calm the monkey down, can rationalize during the ensuing days that the odds are it is not cancer, he's still there, rattling the cage and taunting me. *It could be cancer. Your mother, husband, and grandson all had cancer.*

When the ultrasound takes nearly an hour and it is obvious the technician is concentrating on two specific areas, one on each side, there is no sigh of relief when I'm informed I'll get the results in a few days. No, instead, on the drive home, I'm imagining what it would be like to go through surgery, radiation, and chemotherapy, the same regimen that David endured. *How will you keep working with all that?* the primate taunts. *How will you pay the bills?*

Then tears spring to my eyes as I reflect on how difficult the treatment had been for David, who'd survived cancer only to die of a heart condition five years later, leaving his family much too soon. *My children. My fatherless children!* A gasp escapes me as I wonder how they will handle losing yet another parent. Because, you see, by the time I arrive home from the half-hour drive, the monkey mind has plotted my death and planned my funeral.

The subsequent phone call informing me that one area seems to be of no concern and the other merits a repeat ultrasound in six months does alleviate that imminent worry of death, but I know myself well. When that time frame ends, there's no stopping the monkey. He'll be back, rattling the cage as soon as I'm standing in front of that mammogram machine.

When did this begin, and from where does it stem? I've asked myself that question many times. Was it something hereditary or situational that made me like this? I married a man who'd never experienced a bout of anxiety. He'd laughed when I explained why I wouldn't teach our children the nighttime prayer I'd grown up with: "If I should die before I wake, I pray the Lord my soul to take."

"I worried about dying all the time," I told him. "After my mother left the room, I'd lay there in the dark, wondering. 'If I should die?' Why would I die? Can children die? If I could die, should I even go to sleep? Would my parents die while I slept?"

He'd snorted with laughter at the confession, so I knew he hadn't been the worrywart I'd been as a child. Thank goodness for that—I can't imagine what parenting would have been like if we'd both fretted incessantly about every fever or hesitated pushing our children too high on the swing because they might fall out.

While I'd certainly been a nervous child that grew into an anxious adult, I believe the monkey made his first debut in 1992 during my bout with chronic fatigue syndrome. After months of feeling ill and seeing half a dozen specialists who couldn't tell me what was wrong, my primary doctor essentially washed his hands of me. Alone in bed that night, I began crying. Sobbing quickly escalated to terror. *What is wrong with me? Will I ever find out? Even my own doctor doesn't believe me. What if I never get better? What if the doctor is right and it's all in my head? Am I going crazy?*

Panicked, my heart raced, and I couldn't breathe. I gasped for air, breaking out in a cold sweat, shaking uncontrollably as I lurched through the house searching for David. I thought I was dying. My frightened husband rushed me to the emergency room, where yet another doctor scoffed at my litany of symptoms even while he ordered a shot of something to calm me down.

I'd had the first of what I would discover was a full-blown anxiety attack. I'd experience the same symptoms once more, but I managed to stay home and handle it with David's calming influence.

These incidents were isolated, under circumstances that warranted an extreme reaction. For the most part, anxiety was not a constant in my adult life, nor did everyday worries incapacitate me. I never felt like I needed medication to keep it at bay. The monkey disappeared from my life for many years, making a brief appearance during high-stress periods: when my husband lost his job after my emergency cesarean birth, and again when he was diagnosed with cancer.

My relatively laid-back spouse became my buffer. No longer laughing at my irrational worries, he'd "talk me down" from them. When it came to his cancer, however, I couldn't share my concerns with him. Not when the doctor had made it clear that patients with positive outlooks had better outcomes than those who didn't. Instead, my two oldest children, Dan and Elizabeth, took over talking me down as I delved into dire statistics on the Internet.

Their practice at defusing my anxiety would come in handy during the critical period after their dad's death. Dan and Elizabeth kept a close eye on me, but they weren't there the night I felt the dark waves of panic approaching. *I can't do this! I can't live without him! How can I stand this?* My heart racing, I gulped for air as my throat tightened. *What can I do? Who can I talk to?* I paced the house. I had plenty of people to turn to, despite the late hour. Sisters had given me their phone numbers, saying I could call at any time. Mary and my older children had said the same thing.

Instead, I turned to Facebook at midnight, beseeching friends who were still on that late to urgently pray for me. A single "I'm praying!" calmed me enough to allow me to sleep. I visited my doctor the next morning, requesting medication in case I ever felt like that again. The bottle of pills he prescribed sat in my cupboard, untouched, for more than two years. Just knowing it was there was enough.

I know what it feels like to live a life free of the monkey, for he disappeared again for a few months. I was certain I'd discovered the answer: it was prayer. My Bible studies reinforced the concept of worry denoting a lack of faith. I practiced faith knowing faith can overcome fear. For nearly a year, I surprised myself, my family, and Mary with my complete lack of anxiety.

Get on an airplane for the first time despite that lifelong fear of death? *No big deal.* Lose an agent who was attempting to sell the book I'd been pitching for three years? *Meh. So what?* I shrugged my shoulders and sold the book myself within a week. Book publishing and writing is rife with extreme ups and downs, the kind that might push an anxiety-ridden adult into drinking, but no, I handled it all with grace, by God's mercy.

Then, in January 2013, when my grandson's health took an ugly turn and his cancer diagnosis became a terminal one, that old anxiety returned with a vengeance. Panic replaced peace shortly after an online search for cures for his recurring Wilms' tumor turned up horrifying stories of children's deaths from it. The monkey was back.

I don't remember when I confessed my struggle with anxiety to Mary, or when I learned about hers. How many letters did we write that had hidden that aspect of ourselves? Always wishing to appear strong and capable, I'd concealed my weakness from a lot of people. I do remember the relief and astonishment I felt when I realized we had it in common. Since I've become more open about my own struggle, I've discovered the tendency toward anxiety might run in my family.

During a recent visit with Mary, she fell and hurt her shoulder. She immediately called her husband, Jim, to meet her at the ER. Later at her home, I watched as Jim adjusted an ice pack on her shoulder, then checked an area near her eye where she'd had a spot removed.

"Is it redder than it should be?" she asked.

My heart went out to her as I recognized the worry in her voice. The fall had kicked in Mary's anxiety, the kind that my even-keeled husband used to be able to dispel with a few carefully chosen words, just as Jim does for Mary. He leaned over to study the offending area, patted her hand, and commented, "It looks fine." Mary breathed a sigh of relief. For now, everything was going to be fine. Jim had said so.

I had to turn away from the tender domestic scene for a moment; the reminder of what I had lost was too painful. When I met Mary's eyes, her expression softened. It occurred to me that she often seemed to know exactly what I was thinking.

I'd lost my buffer in David. *But I still had Mary.*

Something unexpected occurred during the time Mary and I worked together on this book. One day on my brother's sunporch, I interrupted her train of thought as she detailed some suggested edits.

"So, did your cancer look like this?" I pointed to a bump near my eyelid. Realizing what I'd just done, I began snickering. A few minutes had passed since we'd discussed the section of the book where she mentioned her skin cancer. That had reminded me of the swelling I'd noticed above my eye just days before. Mary leaned over to look, commenting that perhaps I should see the doctor if it didn't go away. When she turned back to the work at hand, I started laughing.

"What?" Mary smiled as I shook my head, laughing harder. "Tell me."

I could barely speak through the mirth that threatened to convulse me. "Oh no! I'm doing it to you now. What I do to Elizabeth. What I used to do to David. And now that I've told you, no matter what you reply, I'm going to be convinced that you are just saying it to make me feel better. It's the monkey mind. It's ridiculous."

Mary began laughing then, but just as quickly, her face turned serious. Mary doesn't laugh as easily as I do about serious subjects like anxiety.

"No. My skin cancer didn't look like that."

Later, alone in the car on the way home, I laughed out loud as I pondered the exchange. Poor Mary! She understood only too well. How serious her face had become as she'd attempted to calm my anxiety. I smiled again as I remembered her struggle to compose herself so I would believe her. She understood it would take a serious answer to allay my fears. Mary is a true friend.

The idea that she might replace David in the buffer department had never occurred to me before. But it made perfect sense. Outside of my children and siblings, I am closer to Mary than anyone else.

Mary Jedlicka Humston

July 2014:

And just like that, there are only a few hours left of July 2014. The time flies. So cliché, I know, but so true. Tonight, I sit on our glider, in the dark, trying to steep in the insect-song and to quell my anxious heart. Well, actually, the anxiety and pain aren't in my heart area. It's on my left, near my shoulder, fist-sized, and it's here stress lodges. Why here? Yes, I know stress causes ulcers, migraines, heart palpitations, and uneasy digestive systems, but my anxiety lodges here.

If it were my shoulder, I'd say it's from all the burdens I carry—past, present, future—and the ones from all sorts of people who really don't need me to carry them, but I do. But this isn't my shoulder. It's not my lung, but it's close. I don't know anatomy well, so I can't pinpoint it. And yet, here I am feeling it a lot lately. A lot. I can go weeks, months, and rarely feel it. Lately? Lots. Why? Why? Why?

August 2014:

Also, another note of interest—back home, back anxiety!! This is very telling. Being gone for a few days away from stressors—home now, and there it comes back. Sigh. What can I do about this?

November 2014:

Edgy. Tired. Anxious. Chest a slow burn, not the wild, fiery anxiety like sometimes.

As a young child, I was certain turtles lurked in my bedroom, ready to snap off my toes. My only protection? To stay draped in the cotton sheet despite those sultry summer nights in the early 1960s. It didn't matter that the bedding and my pajamas were sweat drenched and that heat stifled my every fearful breath. If my toes somehow got untangled from the protective shield, they were goners. And I needed those toes.

Not too many years later, Grandpa Arlo and Grandma Emma brought back buckeyes from one of their trips. We'd never seen such things. Small and hard like a rock. Brown with a lighter color on one side. Perfect for a closed palm or small pocket. For some reason, I'd deemed mine a good-luck charm. We were admonished: "Now don't eat these. They look like nuts, but they aren't. They taste awful. And they're poisonous to some animals." A charm that was poisonous? Little did that matter to me. I was more excited about having some good luck in my pocket. What grade-schooler couldn't use a little help?

So the buckeye accompanied me to country school. One day, something wonderful happened. A fun accomplishment on the playground? A good grade? Teacher accolades? Whatever it was doesn't matter now, but I do remember knowing that good fortune had to be a result of my buckeye. Without thinking, I scooped it from my pocket and impulsively kissed it as my thanks. Then the word *poison* echoed in my head. Could kissing it poison me? I gagged, ran to the water pump by the school's front steps, and grabbed the handle. I pumped it furiously, my arms flying every which way, waiting, waiting, waiting. Blessed, cool water burst from the spout, and I frantically cupped my hands to catch it. I gulped, swishing it in my mouth and spitting it out, over and over and over. I was sure

I would die. Swish. Spit. Swish. The bell rang. Time for class. One last spit. Would I live? Would I die?

Anxiety followed me during high school when thinness and popularity were recurring concerns. Attending college, teaching, parenting, being involved in a myriad of activities, and experiencing a variety of life challenges created an ebb and flow to the years. Worry was always there, occasionally flaring up, but typically not dogging my every step.

It escalated into full-blown anxiety several years ago. What had followed after me, tagging along without invitation, suddenly generated havoc. A new physical ailment manifested. Whereas before I could handle the anxiety, now I had pain that refused to be banished by sheer determination or willpower. It might appear after a casual conversation. Comments I made were later torn to shreds in my mind as I analyzed if I'd hurt others' feelings. I obsessed over what I said, what I should've said, what I didn't say, and how my innocent words could've been wrongly interpreted. I agonized whether I'd destroyed friendships or encouraged gossip. If I wasn't sure if what someone told me was confidential, I'd become tied up in knots wondering if personal information had been inadvertently divulged. Sometimes I'd stew so much I called people to apologize or arranged a meeting to offer explanations of how I hoped they didn't think I meant this or that. Usually, the aggrieved person had no idea what I was talking about; he or she rarely even remembered what I'd just spent hours fretting over.

A gift or a curse? With my capacity for empathy, another anxiety involved the times that people freely shared their secrets, revealing deeply personal and private information. I could sit next to a stranger and hear her life story within minutes. Once, a casual friend shared her frustrations about a school situation. Midway through our conversation, I assured her I would keep everything confidential (in other words, I wasn't going to run out and blab to the world). I'll never forget what she said then. Her steady look emphasized her words. "Oh, I know that, Mary. I wouldn't be telling you any of this if I didn't already know that."

In the beginning when anxiety roared, I rarely shared my rational or irrational thoughts, assuming I just had a propensity for nervousness and would have to live with it. Embarrassment, too, overrode any attempt to discuss it or to have someone help me understand what was going on. Certainly people would think my feelings were rather strange. I know I did. So I worked hard not only to hide them but to bury them.

It took several years to eventually accept this part of my life. To understand I wasn't alone. To claim it as part of me and not a defect. To feel comfortable sharing my worries. To realize that dealing with them didn't make me weak, unstable, or odd. It made me human, someone who now takes medication for this health problem just like I need to take a daily pill for the rest of my life because cancer destroyed my thyroid. I began slowly sharing more with carefully selected members of my family and friends. It demanded faith on my part, and a strong love and friendship from them, for it was extremely difficult to admit that anxiety of this type resided within me.

I learned coping skills and how to get through the episodes. Exercise, especially yoga, was essential. Journaling was key. If I could write out my feelings, I could own them right then and there, in black and white. It didn't always make them go away, but sometimes it did. Talking things out also helped. I communicated to Jim what I needed from him, and he listened, reassured, and tried to dispel the stranglehold I felt gripped in. As adults, my kids soon grasped how they could assist me, and they've been very supportive, as have many friends and family members.

Of course, it was only natural this topic appeared in letters to Mary. I came to find out she dealt with anxiety, too. How could this be? Both of us? What were the odds? So here we were, sharing yet another aspect of our lives. If we could write about it to each other; if we could reply back with love, reality, assurance; if we could accept each other as we are—then another level of friendship had been reached. A deeper level.

I was one of the featured speakers at a Stories of Healing retreat a few years ago. The bulk of my talk pertained to dealing with cancer and myofascial pain syndrome, but I slipped in a sentence or two about my excessive worrying. I glossed over it, really, but it was a start. For you see, writing this chapter is my first detailed, public admission about dealing with anxiety of any kind, seeking counseling for it in the past, and taking medication.

As I write this, the now-familiar pain has settled in. Not full-blown like usual, but it's making its presence known. Yet if sharing helps even one reader not to feel alone, then the confession of my soul has been worth it. Turtles and buckeyes included.

A Signature Friendship

Mona Rottinghaus

When the back door slammed, I heard my husband, Rick's, heavy footsteps. "Mona, the mail is here."

I hurried to the kitchen, picked it up, and began to sort: junk mail, bills, and what I hoped were birthday cards. I set the bills aside while I ran the "give me" or "buy me" letters through the paper shredder. Settling into a chair with the pile of thick envelopes addressed to me, I read return address labels.

"Yes!" I exclaimed when I discovered the one from Cindy.

My thumbnail slipped under the flap. I tore the envelope open, and out slid a faded purple card with a bunny on the front. I gingerly opened it. The frayed fold barely held together, and the corners looked bent and worn. Two extra pages slipped out, with lines of alternating familiar scripts, mine and Cindy's. This card detailed our friendship over the past twenty-nine years. Smiling, I turned to the back cover. The date, February 3, 1985, took me back to my life as a young mother.

I remembered receiving this birthday card that year. There was a note tucked inside from Cindy letting me know I had failed to sign the card I sent her eight months earlier. The return address identified the mystery sender: me. I was a harried young mother at the time with four children, aged two, three, five, and seven. I made time to remember her birthday, but I had forgotten the small detail of a signature before I stuffed the card into the hastily addressed envelope.

Cindy and I met years earlier at a Fourth of July neighborhood party when we were about nine years old, sharing our sparse treat of sparklers as we played for hours. Five years passed before our paths crossed again. In 1969, I switched to a public high school after I finished at the private grade school, and we became classmates. It didn't take long for us to renew our friendship, and over the next four years, we were almost inseparable. We played basketball, ran track, and were on the same cheerleading squad. Our friendship continued as college roommates. When I left college to get married, Cindy was my maid of honor. A few years later, I was her matron of honor.

I looked at the first date and signature again: Cindy, Ted, and Jenny. I grinned as I reviewed our birthday messages and the dates. I noticed how quickly her signature grew to add three more children, remembering her requested prayer for her infertility issue. The small notations about events over the years sparked memories of rainy seasons, hardships endured, parties attended, and children leaving the nest. I held our histories in my hand, a testimony to our enduring friendship.

For twenty-nine years, we re-sent the beloved card. Some years, it arrived late after a frantic search of our home. "Where did I put it?" But it always came. It was something we could depend on, just as we knew we could depend on each other.

The hardest years of my life were from December 2004 through 2006. Rick and I walked a path with our adult children that challenged me as never before. That December, our daughter was stricken with schizophrenia. Being uneducated about mental illness, we didn't recognize the symptoms. I can still visualize the afternoon I cried into my cell phone and poured my despair out to Cindy. She quietly listened, cried with me, and encouraged me with her promise of prayers. She helped me stand when I was too overwrought to stand alone. Eventually, we received a diagnosis for our daughter after a tumultuous time of multiple hospitalizations and scores of doctors. We moved her home with us to recover and regroup.

She was still in battle with this brain disorder when we learned our daughter-in-law had been diagnosed with cancer. She and our eldest son needed help caring for their newborn daughter and three-year-old son while she underwent surgeries, chemotherapy, and radiation. At the same time, our second son's wife gave birth to Garrett, who had three heart issues, requiring multiple hospitalizations.

I turned to Cindy and my friends with a grocery list of prayer requests. I knew the love, support, and daily remembrances from them would give me the strength to face my goliath of pain, confusion, and exhaustion.

Five months and twenty-seven days after Garrett's birth, I received devastating news in the early morning hours. "Mom, Garrett died this morning."

My shattered heart squeezed so tightly sometimes it was hard to breathe. My circle of friends surrounded me. Their love and prayerful support helped unlock the grief in my heart so I could heal.

Eight years later, I would share the yoke of sorrow with Cindy. Over a lunch date, she shared that her granddaughter would be born in a few months but was not expected to survive more than a few minutes. I knew the anguish felt by a grandmother. I had already lived it. I took her hand and wrapped my arms around her as she prepared to travel the journey no parent wants to take: to mourn the loss of a grandchild and watch your children grieve the death of a child.

"Mona, can you help me find fabric with delicate lilies on it?" Cindy asked one day. "I want to make a quilt to wrap around baby Lily when she is born."

"Sure, I'd love to help."

I searched the Internet but was unable to find the perfect print. "Let me make it for you using my digital garment printer."

"You can do that?"

"I've done it before. Come over and we can design something together."

She came to my house, and we used the graphics program on my computer. When we were finished, we had created her vision of soft green lilies of the valley and the name *Lily Jean* in delicate pink. It matched the previously purchased fabrics perfectly. We dug through my stash and found a piece of lace fabric that was ideal to complete the quilt. We spent the afternoon together and shared the common ache in our hearts.

After Cindy's precious grandchild was born and passed, I assured her I was traveling to the funeral.

"No, it's too far. It's a twelve-hour drive," she said. "That's too much."

"Family and friends drove twelve hours to share in your family's joy," I said, referring to her daughter's wedding years earlier. "Why can't I drive twelve hours to love you in your grief?"

It's what friends do. You go to each other, both in joy and sorrow. As I held Cindy and her husband Ted that day at the funeral, I knew our friendship bond was here to stay. There is a song by Michael W. Smith that states: "A lifetime's not too long to live as friends." Life has taught me this truth, and I have a birthday card to prove it.

Mona Rottinghaus is farm woman, wife, mother, and grandmother in Waterloo, Iowa. She has owned and operated an apparel-decorating business for over twenty years. She enjoys sewing her own clothing, quilting, playing the guitar, writing, and vegetable gardening. She's been published in Love Is a Verb, My Love to You Always, Chicken Soup for the Soul: It's Christmas!, Chicken Soup for the Soul: Just Us Girls, *and* Miracles & Moments of Grace: Inspiring Stories of Survival. *Her current writing projects include an inspirational book on mental illness, anecdotes about family living on an Iowa farm, and her ancestors' love stories. She also volunteers as an educator and support-group facilitator for the National Alliance on Mental Illness organization. Contact Mona at monasoriginals@yahoo.com or monatheoriginal.blogspot.com.*

CHAPTER NINE

Losses

Dear Mary, have you ever lost a friend?

Mary Potter Kenyon

"I'm scared to get too close to him," I confided. "Because of his age."

I didn't have to say any more. Mary knew what I meant. I didn't want to face the possibility of a friend dying. The death of my husband was too recent, and I was raw with grief.

But it was too late. I already loved Cecil Murphey. The fact that I can admit as much shows just how far I have come in the friendship department. I love Shelly Beach, Wanda Sanchez, and dozens of other women I have met through Christian Writers conferences.

Then there's my Bible-study family. I love each and every one of them. "I think that must be what heaven is like," my daughter Elizabeth commented after one of our more animated studies when we'd laughed until we were nearly in tears. I'd agreed. It is exactly how I imagine heaven: a group of people who love the Lord and each other, joking and laughing with ease. There will likely be singing and dancing involved too, except we'll all be good at it then.

It was an unlikely pairing. Cecil ("Cec" to friends) was the same age my mother had been when she died. He was the author of more than a hundred books. More significantly, he was the author (with Don Piper) of one of my husband's favorites, *90 Minutes in Heaven*. The very last book I'd known David to touch was *Getting to Heaven*, another of Cecil's books.

On the night of my husband's wake, I received word that I'd won a scholarship to a June writers' conference in Illinois, courtesy of Cecil Murphey. A few months later, I heard about another writing conference where Cecil would be one of the keynote speakers. With the chance to meet the man behind the scholarship and the author of David's favorite books, I signed on. The aforementioned Shelly and Wanda, who lived in Michigan and were already friends with Cec, made it possible for me to share a dinner table with the man I idolized.

I worried I would become tongue tied or starstruck by the famous author. Instead, I felt an instant connection. Cec was what my husband would have referred to as one of those "real people" he'd always admired. I took several workshops from him at the conference, learning from a master whose advice would come to me, unbidden, years later, even as I worked on this book. At the dinner table, I soaked up the atmosphere, listening to publishing talk between Cec and Shelly. They so effortlessly navigated a world I had not yet become attuned to: editors, agents, and publishers. At the time, just a few months after my husband's death, I could not have imagined in my wildest dreams that I would be signing not one but four book contracts with a publisher over the next three years and be working with my own editor.

On the way to the airport to drop Cec off, I felt drawn to him in a way I wasn't accustomed to feeling toward any man outside of the one I'd been married to for nearly thirty-four years. I listened as Cec talked about his wife, his love for her evident from his almost reverent tone. It was obvious he was eager to get home. I smiled at his words. I'd felt the same when I'd met a Baptist minister across the table at the Illinois conference I'd attended a few months before. As Bill Patterson recounted a summer trip he'd taken with his wife and grandchildren, his eyes sparkled and his gestures became animated. I told him later it was evident how much he loved his family. It reminded me of my own husband. So many at his wake had commented that was how David always spoke of me and the children.

So why did I suddenly feel a stark sadness emanating from Cec? I tried to dismiss it as my own baggage of grief that I carried everywhere. Could it just be he was tired after days of teaching? I studied him closely. Perched on the edge of the back seat, he leaned forward, talking enthusiastically to Shelly and Wanda in front. The man radiated energy. He'd run several miles that morning, a practice he'd confessed to doing daily. When I unbuckled and got out of the van for a proper good-bye, I felt it again as I hugged him. I almost gasped out loud at the deep, sharp sorrow that surrounded him. His body language betrayed nothing as he hurried toward the airport, turning to wave before entering the door.

I asked Shelly about it later. "Why would I have felt a terrible sadness surrounding Cec?"

She surmised it might be residual heartache from his past, and I accepted that.

I believe now it was an omen of what was to come. A few months after that airport hug, Cecil Murphey's wife died. I wondered if God had given me a hint of the pain my new friend was to experience.

Because by then we were friends, I added Cec to the roster of my Tuesday outreach. Since my husband had died on a Tuesday, I used that weekday as a time to reach out to others, healing myself in the process. Cec, Wanda, Shelly—they were all beneficiaries of my ritual, as were half a dozen other people. When Cec learned of my grandson Jacob's terminal diagnosis in January 2013, he promised a daily prayer for Jacob's entire family. When he was in Iowa for a writer's workshop in the summer of 2014, he performed my oldest son's wedding in my brother's beautiful backyard. The same backyard Mary and I would view from their sun-porch months later as we worked on *Mary & Me*.

Unlike Mary, I have not had many friends die. My losses included only two: my best friend, David, and Pam, a long time pen pal I'd never met personally. Pam Pierre answered one of my pen pal requests in a Catholic Natural Family Planning newsletter when I was pregnant with my fifth in 1992. She wasn't Catholic, but she was light-years ahead of me in mothering a large family and in faith. Besides stuffing priority mailers with coupons every month for nearly twenty years, she filled my mailbox with cards and notes that let me know she was praying for me. I saved an email Pam once sent, a prayer for healing when we thought

David's cancer had returned. I also have the last birthday card she sent me in 2011, which was my first birthday without Mom and was also the first anniversary of her death. Along with the card, Pam sent twenty-five dollars toward the cost of the writer's conference Mary and I were going to attend together. Pam lost her son that month in a freak skiing accident. Two weeks later, Pam also died. Despite not ever having met her, I grieved my prayer warrior. I couldn't imagine what her family was feeling in the double loss of loved ones. I thought about them later when I realized I was going to lose a grandchild so soon after I'd lost my mother and husband.

Losing friends is an experience I could do without. But just as the only way a writer can avoid rejection is to never send anything out, the only way I can avoid that particular loss is to never acquire any friends. And now that I know what it is like to have them, I can't bear that thought either. Would I have given up even one minute with David to avoid the grief that followed the loss of him?

I have lost other friends, though not to death. New to this friendship thing, I'm finding it difficult to let go of any close relationship I form, no matter how brief. Just as I have come to do in regards to my transformation of faith, I look to Mary to mentor me through these situations.

"Is it normal to have someone come into your life, seem so important, only to disappear just as quickly?" I ask.

Mary is the expert on these matters, living in a college town where new neighbors and friends come and go. "Sometimes it hurts when we don't know why a friendship dissipates. Other times, it might be someone who was only meant to cross our path for a short while."

Her answer suffices, but just barely. Now that I know how to develop them, I relish my close relationships. I want to gather up potential pals, collecting them for display on a shelf, where I can pull one off when I need him or her. Evidently, I still have much to learn. But then, I have the best teacher around. I have Mary.

Mary Jedlicka Humston

Sometimes it just happens. You look across the table at a woman you've never met. You politely smile and echo a "hello." Her bright eyes and returning smile connect to something within you, and you immediately know she will be more than an acquaintance. You're not surprised when your gut proves correct.

Helen and I were introduced at the opening lesson of a Bible study when she was almost eighty years old and I was forty-four. We attended many more studies and monthly Christian Women's Club luncheons after that. Somewhere along the way, we started chatting on the phone and then meeting for tea and conversation, usually at her home. Our talks covered a multitude of subjects: the past, current events, our faith, and the future. I could count on her prayer-warrior status to ease me through challenges, and I reciprocated by responding to her requests, too.

Upbeat. Encouraging. Lover of McDonald's fish sandwiches and fries. Sharer of tea, books, magazines, and faith. Looking from the outside, one might call her my mentor, but she wasn't. She was my friend. In those twelve years of friendship, she lived a full, vibrant life until a second fall and a broken bone sent her to a local adult retirement community. First, she moved to an independent living apartment. Then she transitioned to an assisted living apartment. And, finally, she required the health center after a stroke.

She wasn't doing well right before Jim and I left on a trip. Shortly after returning, the dreaded call came. My journal entry tells it all.

June 24, 2010:

> Helen was in such bad shape after her stroke, so I can't be sad for
> her. She's not in pain. And dear, sweet Helen is with the heavenly
> host and with her family and other loved ones who've passed on
> before her. In that sense, I'm happy for her. But I'm sad for all of
> us left behind; those sweet eyes will never gaze at me again.
>
> Helen, you were a dear friend. My life was richer for knowing
> you. And while I know I'll cry a lot today, and in the days to
> come, I'm crying for me, not you. You are free of the ill con-
> fines of your body, and you are happy and joyous in peace, good
> health, and ecstasy! Instead of "God be with you," now I can say
> (truly) that God is with you in the full afterlife experience. Peace,
> my friend, peace.

I am no stranger to grief and dying, having attended many wakes, vis-
itations, memorial services, and funerals. But that doesn't make death any
easier. Both sets of grandparents and several aunts and uncles have passed
away. And my husband's parents died far too young. His dad suffered a
sudden, massive heart attack when Jim and I were only thirty-one years
old. Ten years later, his mom endured three and a half months from lung
cancer diagnosis to death. We still feel the emptiness of their absence. We
are still grieving the loss of family and friends. Both are difficult beyond
words.

One of my first older friends was Henrietta, whom I met when she
was close to ninety years old and I was twenty-two. We were members of
Triangle Arts Club, an organization in Bellevue that celebrates art, music,
and literature. In an interesting twist, the former English instructor had
been in the same position at the very school where my English teaching
career had begun.

After living in Bellevue over five years, Jim, one-year-old Jill, and I
moved to Iowa City. I returned many times, always making sure to visit

Henrietta, who by that time lived in the local care facility. Out of all the four-hour round trips I made, we only missed seeing her once.

On the day of our final visit, she perked up when we arrived. I knew she wasn't feeling well, so we didn't stay long. The girls, no older than five and three at the time, were delighted to see their drawings hanging on Henrietta's closet doors. I remember changing Jonathan's diaper on her bed while Jill and Elizabeth played in her tiny bedroom and hung onto the chair arms where Henrietta half-sat, half-slept. That was the last time we saw her.

I had a strong need for socialization after the correct diagnosis and medication for myofascial pain syndrome improved my quality of life in 2001. Because the lingering side effects of that illness had precluded having a job, it was only natural I gravitated toward clubs and organizations that met during the day when I could work around my still-limited energy and family time. The majority of women in these groups were in their sixties and beyond while I was in my forties, allowing me the unique pleasure of making many new friendships that enriched my life immeasurably, but it also meant saying some inevitable good-byes.

It isn't just elderly friends I have lost. There's Teresa, a high school classmate. Several years ago, Jim and I attended her outdoor wedding at Munsinger Gardens along the Mississippi River in St. Cloud, Minnesota. As soon as we located the gardens and parked, I opened the car door to hear familiar laughter. Forty years dropped away, and we were just Jed and Bitt (our high school nicknames) hugging in the parking lot, she in her wedding gown, looking radiant.

I would be reminded of that day a few years later when she wrote me a long letter about her newly diagnosed cancer. How do I encapsulate her cancer journey into mere paragraphs? I can't. Teresa's dying brought classmates Karlene, Virginia, and me to stand at her bedside with her husband, Neil. We'd canceled two other visits prior to this one because she hadn't felt well. If only we'd have known that those were her good days. Now, here we were at last, and she was unable to respond. What did she hear as we shared memories of getting dressed before dances at her house, the slumber parties, and stories about her and Karlene editing the newspaper? Even in the midst of sadness, we laughed with her and told her how much we loved her. It was a hallowed time, insulated in that twilight time of dying as we shared tears, "I love yous," and words of endearment and friendship for the final time.

Karlene, Virginia, and I met again several days later, this time for the funeral. The spirit of our fun-loving, boisterous friend Teresa nestled among us as we sat in the pew during her funeral Mass, together one last time.

Loss will gut-punch you no matter the age of the deceased. It drops you to your knees. It shatters the dreams of your families, especially those of grandchildren and great-grandchildren who lose the chance of getting to know their elder. It brings tears, anger, shock, and a rejection of faith— or the complete opposite: a reliance on faith.

It creates the walking wounded.

Mary and I wrote copious letters when she experienced her mother's lingering illness and death. I offered solace and prayers before, during, and after her mother passed away in November 2010.

But I'll never forget her call in March 2012 when David unexpectedly died. My cell phone was turned off while I attended a meeting. Poor Mary had to leave her devastating news on voicemail.

In one sudden moment, her world turned upside down. I drove the three-hour round-trip to David's visitation to provide what comfort I could. It felt so meager and inadequate, but I hoped my presence was helpful. I returned home that night. The next day, Jim and I traveled back and attended David's funeral.

Mary was blessed to have her children and siblings nearby who administered wonderful support. What could I do when I lived farther away? Write letters, of course. And that's what I did.

Because Mary was writing me when she discovered David had died in his nearby chair during the night, I worried our letter writing might

falter. Would she resent me? How in the world would we resume our correspondence after such sad circumstances? I sensed she could use some
normalcy in her daily life, so I filled her mailbox with letters. We continued our recitations of what we were doing, how she and the kids were
handling grief, what kept us busy, and our writing endeavors. I allowed
her to grieve in whatever way she needed and let her set the tone, but
never hesitated to ask how it felt to lose David, to become a member of a
club no one wanted to join: the widow club.

At least once a month, I drove to Manchester, where we began the
routine of eating at a local tearoom, talking as we polished off their tasty
fruit, nut, and lettuce salad with the special dressing we both loved. As
with our letters, I let Mary steer the conversation. Talk about our writing? Okay. Talk about weight challenges? Car problems? The kids? Okay.
Other times, I asked about her worst moments, or how she possibly could
stand her deep loss, relentless day after relentless day. I tried to imagine
what it would feel like to be her. What would I want to talk about? I knew
if I crossed a line, Mary would tell me. We were close friends, and we both
knew she could refuse to reply.

Afterward, we usually browsed in her sister Pat's nearby consignment
shop, which typically yielded an antique lamp or two for me. It got to the
point of absurdity when I'd see one I just had to have, despite having no
idea where I'd put it at home. Jim humored me until seven lamps later;
even I realized there was no room for more unless I took to hanging them
from the ceilings. Was this my way of trying to bring light into the darkness of sorrow? One day, lamps no longer called my name.

If Mary and I still had time left, we'd take a walk, chat with her children, or go to the cemetery, but always, we would talk. One day, we'd
scored some good sales at a nearby Hallmark store. As we got into my
Escape, something tickled us. I wish I could remember what. All I know is
I laughed so hard, the only sounds coming out of me were sharp wheezes,
like a dog hoarse from hours of annoying barking. I couldn't stop.
Neither could Mary.

Occasional laughter was healing after David's death, especially since it wasn't the only stress happening at the time. She'd had earth-shocking news fifteen months before.

December 2010

Dear friend Mary, whose husband and mother were blindsided by cancer, just called, and she's on the way to UI Hospital with her daughter Beth and five-year-old grandson Jacob, just diagnosed with cancer today! I can't even cry yet, the news is too fresh, but already my heart's breaking for what I know is still ahead for Mary, Jacob, Beth and Ben, and the rest of their families.

Letters also sustained us during Jacob's long cancer journey. While David's death was sudden, Jacob's was not. Our correspondence and visits continued while he endured different treatments, remission, recurrences, and a trial study that didn't produce the return to health as hoped and prayed for. Jacob died shortly after his eighth birthday.

I can't even begin to imagine losing a mother, husband, and grandson in the span of three years, but that's what happened to Mary. Writing sustained her, so it was no surprise she poured her heartbreak into a book that has helped countless people in their grief.

I stumbled upon this quote by Alexandra Stoddard recently: "Life is to be celebrated, not merely lived. Today is the time; here, where we are, is the place." If I've learned anything about loss, it's that we, the living, must honor our loved ones by embracing life to the fullest, because only God knows what is just around the corner.

Roll Model

Kristi Paxton

A surprise awaited me in an old gym-turned-community center in 1983. Phyl danced in the front row, and I claimed the back as we mimicked the moves of a glamorous Jazzercise expert. I was thirty years old, and Phyl was fifty-three, just a few years younger than I am today. *How can that old lady do all these moves when I can't keep up?* I immediately chose her for my role model.

"How long have you been doing Jazzercise?" she asked me as we finished our workout, grabbed our bags, and headed outside. After each class, our talk time increased. Eventually, we finished longer chats at coffee shops with cups of black coffee—the first of many addictive cups we would share the next few decades.

We had nothing in common other than a deep, near-religious devotion to caffeine. She was old. I was young. She loved cats. I adored dogs. She was a devout Lutheran, I a doubtful Baptist. She was Republican. I was a mutt-like mix of political ideology, but definitely not Republican.

Phyl's kids were grown-ups. I hadn't yet started a family when we met, but she later watched my growing belly at Jazzercise, encouraging me to continue my fitness program. She was with me on her fifty-fifth birthday, the same day my baby was stillborn, the day I came home empty handed. Few words were spoken, but she was there. Always there.

Long and lean, Phyl watched me struggle to get my stocky body back into pre-pregnancy condition. We added bicycling to our Jazzercise dates.

She was a natural cyclist. My love of biking didn't blossom, but when you pick a role model, you do what the model does. A year and a day later, when I gave birth to a healthy son, occasional bike dates kept us in touch.

When my son was two, Phyl helped me load him onto a baby bike seat and haul him to Dike, an Iowa town ten miles away. The photo she took with her disposable camera is still one of my favorites—my oversized '80s hairdo flying out behind me, a big smile on my face. My tagalong son in his round Styrofoam helmet leaned around me to get a glimpse of the road ahead.

"What are we going to do when it snows and we can't bike anymore?" Phyl asked one day after a ride.

"Cross-country ski!" I quipped, half-joking.

Within the week, she'd bought skis.

Two years later, I added a daughter to the expedition. You could sometimes see the three of us following Phyl on ski trails winding through Black Hawk Park in Cedar Falls. I'd plop my baby girl in a backpack and pull my two-year-old son on a wooden sleigh. It was more grunt-shuffling than skiing, but Phyl told me I was the most durable person she knew. I still cherish that compliment.

Our conversations did not focus on husbands or kids. Though I loved them dearly, mine might as well have been sacks of flour that I schlepped through time and space. For with Phyl, I was not someone's mom or wife. Our fun times were about us, about me, and that is when it occurred to me that she was teaching me about true-blue friendship—understanding and appreciation. Encouragement. Our bond was visceral, garnished with laughter, and topped with hot coffee. We made no judgments.

By 2004, Phyl was an avid bicyclist. She talked me into registering for TRIRI, Touring Ride In Rural Indiana. "Since you haven't been training, let's take a practice hill ride, so you'll be ready for Indiana," she said. She knew my bike was dusty, still hanging where I'd stored it last season. She understood from personal experience the following weeks' five hundred miles of Indiana hills would be ruthless.

"Sure. You plan it, and I'll show up," I said without enthusiasm.

After the first few miles of our practice ride, we stopped to snap a photo from a bluff above a velvet valley between Wadena and Elgin, Iowa.

"This is the most beautiful spot on the planet!" I exclaimed. Shortly after that, I lost my groove. In biker lingo, I bonked. Sun, headwinds, and humidity bore down on us. And then, the beauty simply disappeared.

An endless series of slopes separated the tiny towns where we filled my empty water bottles. I struggled. Phyl noticed my sweaty pallor, so between burgs, she poured water from her bottles into mine. Encouragement is the fabric of her personality, and Phyl used it to wave me forward.

"I can't believe how great you're doing, especially since this is your first ride of the season," she proclaimed. She should have said, "You big wimp. Why didn't you train? You are going to die in Indiana!"

I whined, but Phyl remained positive. She made me laugh, reminding me that in cycling—as in life—you must have one horrendously ugly day to propel you through future bad days. Then you can say, "At least this isn't as bad as that hellish day in Iowa's Little Switzerland." Phyl gently prodded me to climb onto life's grand roller coaster.

Somehow I survived the Indiana ride later that summer. My memories include slipped chains, near dehydration, drenching rains, and some of the best food and state park lodges in the United States. I began to appreciate the thrill of the roller coaster.

When I was fifty-two, I wanted to abandon my secure job with benefits for the uncertainty of freelance writing and substitute teaching. A gem among naysayers, Phyl encouraged me to fly. After I quit my job and began to write, she'd often reach into her bike bag and extract a carefully clipped copy of a newspaper article I'd written. Sometimes, she included a bonus comic strip, making me take time to laugh.

Phyl became tour guide to a small group of cyclists and signed us up for a weeklong route through Iowa, Wisconsin, and Minnesota. On the eve of our 2009 tri-state trip, I had failed to pack. My bike tires were flat. I called Phyl. Crabby and out of shape, I groped for an excuse. "I've misplaced all my biking shorts. I don't think I can go."

"Don't worry. I packed extra shorts," Phyl answered, "and I'm sure Lila will loan you her bike." So reluctantly, I showed up, and predictably, we had fun, laughing and singing our way through the rolling hills of those three states. The hard hills were sprinkled with tiny towns offering remarkable pieces of pie—and coffee, of course.

Today, Phyl is eighty-one years old. She still puts between five and ten thousand miles on her bicycle yearly—even in Iowa, where we have long months of snow and ice. Sometimes when she convinces me to ride, I catch myself wondering, *What will happen when mortality catches up to one of us? Will it end on a horrible hill where an aging heart will finally say "No more" and a limp form will crumble to the pavement, releasing the lively spirit it once held?* Then I envision Phyl tenderly pulling my body to the soft grass beside the road. She will look down into my face and say, "Nice final bonk."

Phyl's story did not end as I predicted. In May 2014, just a few months after she helped organize my sixtieth birthday party, and days after a lengthy bike ride, Phyl was diagnosed with cancer: four kinds, final stages. She refused my offer to take a series of short bike rides to coffee shops.

"Why would I want to do short rides? What I loved about riding were the long hills, the challenges," she said. I encouraged her to ride her cancer like a ridiculously long hill, and she gave it her best.

Minutes before she closed her eyes for what would be the last time, Phyl and I whispered a celebration of our precious friendship to each other. Her extraordinary heart continued to beat with athletic performance for many days until the moment she finally slipped away on July 22, 2014. She was eighty-three years old. Today, I can smile and reflect upon the fun spots that would not have dotted my dull life story without Phyl.

Kristi Paxton was a postmaster for twenty-six years. Now a freelance writer, her features appear in the Waterloo-Cedar Falls Courier *and University of Northern Iowa's UNIBusiness Alumni Magazine. When not writing, Kristi is a substitute teacher in Northeast Iowa. She splits her time between a house in the Iowa woods and an old boat in North Carolina. Two grown children, husband Denny, and puppy Smalls complete Kristi's family portrait. Contact her at kristi.a.paxton@gmail.com, or see her blog at kristipaxton.tumblr. com.*

CHAPTER TEN

Faith

Dear Mary, tell me about your faith.

Mary Potter Kenyon

T he idea for this book seemed to come from nowhere. When I looked across the room at Mary during a speech, I'd felt that jolt of electricity, a very real sense that what I was about to say was not coming directly from me.

As soon as I blurted out that my next book was going to be one co-written with Mary, I wondered at the assertion. This revelation came as a surprise. Wasn't my next project about utilizing creativity in every-day life? Hadn't I done presentations on that very topic, and developed a framework for just such a book? Sure, I might not have gotten any further than generalized notes and a rough outline. It had been months since I'd worked on anything new. But a book with Mary? Where had that idea come from? Yet as soon as I said it, I knew it was the direction God wanted me to go.

God? It seems a bit bold, and somewhat pretentious, to declare one's writing to be inspired by God, doesn't it? I'd once heard a Christian agent declare that the worst line he'd ever been approached with was, "You're going to be my agent. God told me." He'd stopped listening to the pro-spective client as soon as he heard that. Apparently one can go too far in proclaiming divine inspiration and direction.

Let me explain. I haven't always thought this way. In fact, if anyone had asked me even five years ago who was the more devoted Catholic or the better Christian between the two of us, I would have answered (somewhat self-righteously, I might add) that I was, because I believed and followed the "boxed church rules." Because birth control is a sin and only males should be allowed to be priests, and anyone who disagreed was a buffet-style Catholic, picking and choosing which beliefs to follow. Like my old prerequisite requirements for potential friends, I am ashamed to admit I held a very rigid, compartmentalized view of what constituted a good Catholic. As for those self-avowed "Christians," I was certain the term was likely an oxymoron and that the majority of them were anything but.

Let me take this opportunity now to apologize to each and every genuine Christian, especially my dear friend Mary.

"Should we pray first?" Mary asks each time we've gotten together to work on our book. Mary is the one who requested a prayer from a faith-filled friend for us to share at each meeting. Mary sends me copies of inspiring quotes and Bible verses that seem to reach me just when I need them. Mary has taught me so much more about being a Christian than I could ever teach her.

My mother, a devout Catholic, died on my birthday in November 2010. That night I emailed a woman who had become a prayer warrior for me, one of those self-avowed Christians I hadn't been so sure of. Beth had reconnected with me just a few months before, finding me on Facebook as her husband lay in a hospital bed, dying of the same cancer my mother had just been diagnosed with.

"I feel like such a failure as a daughter," I wrote her. "My mom died without me being where she wanted me to be, faith-wise. I must have been such a disappointment to her. I couldn't be the Catholic she wanted me to be."

"Why does your mother's faith experience have to be yours?" Beth replied. "Your mother reached heaven her way. That was her journey. You can find your own way."

I could find my own path to heaven? It didn't have to be the scapular-wearing, rosary-carrying, straight and narrow, doctrinal and ritualistic path my mother had followed? Beth's words were eye opening and very freeing.

The summer after my mother died, in response to reading notebooks she'd left behind with the repeated admonition for her children to utilize their God-given talents, I decided to honor her by doing just that. I would acknowledge that I had a natural talent for writing and begin taking it seriously.

As the perfect first step, I signed up for my first writer's workshop, a Christian one held in Cedar Falls, Iowa. I wasn't sure what to expect, but I do remember that upon my arrival, I stood outside the closed door of the conference center for a very long time, bracing myself for what would surely be disappointment on the other side.

I entered the building with a huge chip on my shoulder: the distrust of women in general, particularly those who called themselves "Christian." I didn't expect their warm welcome. By the end of the first day, I still wasn't sure of the genuineness of the religious fervor of some of the workshop leaders or attendees. By the end of the second day, I knew they had something I didn't. I'd lived a good, decent life and loved the Lord, but I hadn't managed to forge the personal relationship with Him that these women seemed to have. Their heartfelt, spontaneous praying appealed to me more than anything. I would write as much to Mary:

> I couldn't believe how nice these women were. They truly are the epitome of Christian faith. I've never seen such openness. And their prayers! They weren't rote prayers, or memorized. Their prayers came from their heart. This is the first time I've ever heard such praying. I want to be able to pray like that.

I walked into a room full of strangers the first day of that workshop, and three days later, I left with something I hadn't managed to obtain in the previous thirty years: several fledgling female friendships.

A few months later, Mary would accompany me to Kansas for my second Christian writer's conference. It would be the first time we'd been alone together for longer than an hour or two. The experience turned out to be both creatively and spiritually inspiring. Certain God had sent me there to sell my couponing book, I was confused when that wasn't happening. There were so many interesting workshops to choose from that my head was reeling. When I confided as much to Mary on that last morning, she asked if she could pray for me. Then she took hold of my hands and began praying. Out loud. From the heart. Head down, her eyes closed, she'd missed my look of amazement.

"Mary?" I ventured afterward. "You know how to pray like that? I didn't know."

It was then Mary confessed how much my words about "seeing such faith-filled women for the first time" had hurt her, how she'd wondered how she'd failed to be a Christian example in all those years of writing me. What had she done wrong, or failed to do?

That was my first inkling that letters might not convey all the nuances of a person's life the way personal visits would.

Why had I not seen it? Suddenly, so many things she'd written made sense. I was instantly ashamed. When Mary would write that she needed to pray about something in order to discern God's will for her (because she'd said as much many times), I'd actually thought she was looking for a way out, an excuse to say no to me about a request or event. Because how could I argue with God if the decision had been His? Instead, she truly had been discerning what direction God wanted her to go.

When she'd mentioned how she'd prayed for her children's future mates ever since they were young, I'd found it quaint and old-fashioned. When she'd talked about her many church activities, Bibles studies, and retreats, I'd considered those things a handy excuse for socializing.

Why had I failed to realize the depth of Mary's faith despite all those letters? She'd certainly done her best to share it. The answer came to me in the midst of my own faith journey, one that seemed to begin the night my mother died and was jump-started when I lost David seventeen months later.

Why hadn't I seen it?

Simple. I wasn't looking.

According to Jeremiah 29:13 in the Bible, "You will seek me and find me when you seek me with all your heart" (NIV). It wasn't about Mary at all. It was about me. It wasn't until my mother's death that I began actively seeking God. I didn't see Mary's Christian example because I hadn't yet developed spiritually. I wasn't "there" yet. I didn't recognize true faith because I didn't have my own. Just as my relationship with Mary deepened after David's death, so did my relationship with God. It was through the darkness of loss that I discovered the true light of the world.

Now I see it. I see Mary's deep faith. But even better? I share it.

Mary Jedlicka Humston

Mary and I never spent long periods of time together without children and spouses. Our first big outing was to a writer's conference in Kansas. It cemented our friendship.

To say that Mary stunned me when she hadn't seen my faith in our correspondence is an understatement. I was not only hurt but shocked that my witness was that shallow or, worse, so unapparent that she saw it first in the women at the Cedar Falls workshop before she saw it in me. Second-guessing myself, I wondered what I had done wrong or failed to do. Did I write too many complaints or whine too much? Our letters were safe havens for that type of intimate sharing. I also knew I'd written about Bible studies, scripture, prayer, and all the church activities that were near and dear to me. How could that have come across as insignificant in our thousands of letters?

It was a wake-up call I could learn from. God had work to do, or else that important part of me would've been obvious to Mary. I'll be the first to admit I'm not perfect (no, it's true) and not all my actions are those of a faith-filled person, though God knows I've tried my best. Isn't that all that any of us can aspire to? To pray for guidance as we travel the challenges along the road?

So that's what I did. I sought God's guidance about Mary's new revelation. It took prayer, discernment, and time before I broached the topic in Kansas, since I didn't think I could fully convey it in a letter. And God guided us to a meaningful conversation which deepened an already-strong friendship that now included an even stronger faith.

My journey of faith began at birth. I am deeply grateful that I grew up in a churchgoing family. One Sunday morning in the 1960s, we were on our way to Mass. Our light-colored station wagon containing my parents and seven of us kids blended with whiteout snow conditions. We met a similarly-colored cream truck (by that I mean a large truck hauling cream) at a four-way country intersection with no stop signs. I sat in the back, my eyes closed, resting my head on the seat, knowing we had a good drive ahead of us. When the cream truck broadsided us, I flew into the middle seat, clueless as to what had happened. The vehicles skidded on the icy gravel road before sliding into the ditch, side by side. After several moments of stunned silence, my family slowly piled out of the car. An imminent visit to the doctor thankfully revealed no major injuries but also prevented church attendance. Dad made sure to call the priest to explain our absence.

I grew up during the pre–Vatican II era of the Catholic Church, and I have to admit I viewed God as stern and remote. When Vatican II hit, I was too young to fully comprehend that windows opened, fresh air blew in, and new attitudes entered. Despite the rejuvenated life flowing around, doubts and questions followed me to college.

I was bombarded by Christians my first semesters on campus. That's the best way I can describe it. There were Christian girls in the dormitory. A mute busboy handed me a brief testimony on a card at the restaurant where I waitressed. Fellow classmates invited me to Bible studies (What? Who studied the Bible?), prayer groups, and retreats.

My faith was private and personal, but God opened my heart. Or did He splay it wide? I saw peace emanating from these individuals who spoke unashamedly about their faith, an inner peace I lacked. It took time to reach the point where I recognized I wanted something more from my faith than what I had. Shortly after turning nineteen, I had that awakening, a born-again experience, a recommitment, if you will. Sitting under a pine tree on campus, I opened my heart, and my blessed but humbled life hasn't been the same since. I loved the verse John 10:10: "I have come that you might have life and have it more abundantly."

"Abundantly" has been the key word. Faith is a lived-out and lived-in essential aspect of my life. I dread imagining where I'd be without it. What paths would I have taken? What type of person would I be? How would I have gotten through the dark days without the light of faith? Certainly I will never be able to understand many circumstances and why they did or didn't happen. My anguish over the shadowed times in life still makes me question why certain events occurred.

Yet God's guidance is never ending. It has been the groundwork of *Mary & Me*. We leapt out in faith when we decided to cowrite, and every step of the way has been met with unified prayer. What chapters should we have? Go to prayer. Who do we ask for guest essays? Go to prayer. Who do we seek for promotional endorsements, blurbs, and our foreword? Again, go to prayer.

One day, I noticed a friend on Facebook offering to write blessings for anyone for any reason. All she requested were a few details about the situation. So I privately messaged Marsha Schupbach Lowe to ask if she'd create one for us while we worked on the book. I was surprised by her quick reply and how appropriate her blessing was:

> Bless this paper, bless this pen.
> Bless this friendship, now and then.
> Place your hand upon this book.
> Bless our readers as they look . . .
> into this precious gift of love.
> All glory be to God above.

I have read the blessing prayer almost every time I worked on this book, and Mary and I read it together whenever we met to work.

Shortly after submitting our proposal and waiting for a reply, I took a walk on a two-and-half-mile trail circling a lake south of town. I'd walked and biked this trail hundreds of times.

Few people were out that quiet, early morning. As I rounded a bend, something to the left among the overgrown bushes, trees, and weeds caught my eye. I slowed down. A face came into view. Then a head. And soon, five to seven well-camouflaged deer appeared. The fawns ignored me, but the adults openly stared. I stared back. Their tails swished as we watched each other for several minutes. Some bent to eat. Unafraid, they remained there while I walked backward to keep them in sight for as long as possible.

Never before had I seen a hint of a deer by this trail. Never.

I knew I'd been gifted. When I'm feeling low, troubled, or needing guidance to make a decision, occasionally God will strategically place meaningful spiritual symbols or signs. For Mary, it might be coins with specific dates, blue butterflies, or stationery discovered at a thrift store. For me, deer and eagles along my path have often given me encouragement. Their presence says to me, "All will be well. Be at peace."

Seeing the unexpected deer didn't signal the publisher would say yes, but I walked on knowing no matter what happened, everything would work out. And it did. The publisher obviously accepted our proposal. This book is the proof. But if he hadn't, Mary and I would've sent out other queries. The book project wasn't to be abandoned. That was clearly a message from above, too.

Deer. Soaring or perched eagles. A stunning sunset. Butterflies. Coins. Random acts of kindness. Smiles from a passerby. Scripture verses that pop out of the Bible in new ways. Just the right words an aching heart needs from a well-placed individual. Surely God is among us. God is in life. God guides.

I feel blessed that Mary and I share faith as another cohesive aspect of our friendship.

Mail Call

Jonna Statt

Who doesn't like to get the mail each day? Amidst the bills and catalogs, it's always fun to receive a letter. Yet in today's high-tech, fast-paced world, we are getting fewer of them.

I live in rural southwest New York. Two of my friends are postmasters in different areas. Both have verified that the volume of mail going into our boxes is down one-fourth from what went in last year, and is half of what went in five years ago. Less junk mail may be a good thing to most people, but fewer letters?

With the proliferation of texts and emails, we are losing that personal touch that only an actual letter can bring. Many of us enjoy books consisting of old letters from famous and not-so-famous people. Can you envision wanting to read a book of someone's texts or emails?

Well, there is a small group of women from around the world who wish to buck this electronics-saturated trend in their own small way and continue to establish and maintain friendships through letters. I am one of them.

"You're a lot like your dad." I have heard this on and off throughout the years. During those typical find-your-own-identity teenage years, I cringed whenever I heard that. In the past several years, I have found it a high compliment, as my dad is such an active, caring person. And he wrote letters—lots of them.

They say that what you grow up with is normal for you, so I thought everyone's dad took trips to the post office after work each day (often accompanied by me). From around the world, Dad managed to make contacts related to his hobbies. These were kept up via writing letters as well as sending packages. I grew to love our large historic post office with its massive doors, extremely high ceilings, and walls that echoed with the sounds of both postal employees and customers. The outgoing mail slots on the side wall fascinated me as a little girl—portals to faraway places I had only read about.

Through one of his British contacts, Dad found me my first pen pal when I was eleven, a girl named Jean in England. I don't remember much of the content of those letters, but I do remember writing back within twenty-four hours each time her much-awaited letters came.

When I was twelve, my address was printed in the Pen Pals section of a teen-genre magazine as a fan of a music group popular in the mid-'70s. Dad had told me if my submission was actually printed, he would finance the stamps for my replies. I often wonder if he secretly regretted that promise, as I received over 200 letters from around the world—and I answered every one of them.

Talk about waiting for the mail! The highest number of letters I received in a single day was thirty-three. Outside of school, meals, and sleeping, I was always writing letters and riding my bike to the post office to mail them. Some of these girls became close friends in the years that followed. Even though our interests may have changed in the interven-ing years, I still am in touch with a couple of those women from over thirty years ago.

Back then, as well as now, pen pals often exchanged what are called "friendship booklets" along with their letters. These handmade booklets are created either for yourself or a friend. You put your own address label and hobbies on the next open space, and then mail it to someone else who then does the same. The last person to sign then sends the full booklet (that has traveled around the world) to whoever it was made for. You can write to people who have signed before you, while others signing after you may do the same. Friendship booklets brought new friends with different interests as I progressed through high school. One ended up living only an hour away, so we visited each other for overnights. (She just recently "found" me again after a thirty-year lapse.)

While busy in college, I didn't seek new pen pals, but I kept writing to the same ones. These friendships continued even after I got married in 1984.

Life after marriage got busier with finishing college, part-time jobs, and many moves. I then stayed at home when my first son was born in 1991. I found myself with extra time during his lengthy naps, so I decided to join International Pen Friends, a still-functioning organization that, for a fee, will connect you with several other women worldwide with similar interests.

Fast forward to today. I have been married for thirty years, had seven children along the way, and still write letters in much of my spare time to thirty-five women worldwide.

These friends range in age from nineteen to eighty-eight, and are single, married, and divorced. They are from all walks of life, including a waitress, a physician, a teacher, a lobster fisherman's wife, orchestra musicians, both 911 and suicide hotline operators, homemakers, widows, and others. They come from the United States, Canada, Japan, Australia, Germany, all of the United Kingdom, Italy, Seychelles, Denmark, Norway, Sweden, Finland, Spain, South Africa, Greece, and more.

My letter friends are like extended family to me. We have shared each other's successes, joys (marriage, birth), challenges (illnesses, job loss, moves), and sorrows (divorce, death of a spouse or child, or even abandonment). I strongly want to be there to talk, listen, encourage, and, yes, pray for each of these friends.

My Christian faith is something very precious to me that I didn't grow up with. It was like an undiscovered treasure that had been waiting for me all along to find. It colors who I am—how I think, feel, and react. It continues to give me a sense of compassion and concern for others.

My pen friends encompass a myriad of beliefs: atheist, agnostic, Catholic, Protestant, Jehovah's Witnesses, Mormon, Wiccan, and even an occultist. I have never wanted anyone I correspond with to feel like a project that I am trying to work on to become just like me. It is good for me to learn about other people's beliefs, lives, and experiences. I let each totally set the pace concerning whatever subjects they would like to discuss in our letters, and I respond honestly whenever asked about my faith. I am just glad to be a friend to anyone, anywhere.

Someone once chided me years ago when hearing of my latest aspirations and projects: "Jonna, you can't change the world." Maybe not, but with the Lord's help I'll try to change my little corner of it. Perhaps my letter friends are a part of God's plan for my life. In return, I have received so much encouragement and joy from them. I wish I could give them all a collective hug in person.

Do you have a little time on your hands? Could you make time to brighten someone's life through a handwritten letter? Then what are you waiting for? Go find those undiscovered, new best friends.

Jonna Statt lives with her teacher husband, Mike, in Andover, New York, along with five of her seven children. Two unclaimed cats and two very strange-looking guinea pigs also call this home. She has a bachelor's degree from Empire State College. When not writing letters, she is probably homeschooling, selling part time on eBay, or deeply enjoying attending classical music concerts and learning to play Bach on her cello. She always has room for one more pen friend. Contact her at jonnafromny@cleaninter.net.

CHAPTER ELEVEN

Sex, Drugs, and Rock & Roll: What We Don't Talk About

Dear Mary, have you ever talked about . . . ?

Mary Potter Kenyon

"Can I ask you something really personal?"

Mary's nervousness amused me. I couldn't imagine anything she might ask that would offend me or hurt our relationship, and yet she was obviously hesitant to broach this subject. We'd just spent the last hour discussing topics that had somehow remained off limits in a friendship spanning nearly three decades.

We'd agreed that politics topped the list. Even during election years we'd barely touched on it, though I had a vague idea who Mary might have voted for once or twice. The subject had never been dubbed taboo; it just wasn't something we discussed in letters. Frankly, during the years when I had struggled just to survive, politics wasn't on my radar at all. That was embarrassing to admit to someone like Mary, who seemed to take her voting privileges seriously. My husband had always voted, and never quite understood when I chose not to. It was a personal failing I wasn't eager to share. Occasionally, my stance had been more of a default position. I couldn't in good conscience vote for a candidate who supported abortion, so I wouldn't vote at all that year. Other times I voted for an underdog candidate, knowing full well they wouldn't win. When I did declare a party, it was Republican.

What else didn't we talk about besides politics? "Well, I've always hesitated to talk to you about my problems or worries regarding homeschooling," I'd ventured. My failure to confide much on that particular topic was shrugged off by Mary.

"All mothers worry about aspects of their school choices," she'd said.

You mean all mothers have those moments when they lay awake at 3:00 a.m. worrying about their children? I wondered. *I could have shared the burden of a late reader, or a daughter who got lost in math, and not worried about being judged for my educational choice?*

"Food stamps. There were times in my marriage when we had to resort to food stamps, and I could never tell you," I blurted out, my face warming with shame. I scrutinized hers for a hint of judgment or disdain. There was none. Instead, she reached across the table and put her hand over mine.

"I knew from your letters that there were times when you really struggled financially."

Was there anything Mary didn't know about me that would have shocked her? I'd racked my brain for other topics we'd never discussed. Did Mary know I still felt conflicted about her strongly held conviction that women should be allowed to become priests? Yes, it turned out she did. That I didn't agree with the medical establishment on the need for a yearly flu shot? Ditto. She knew about that, as well. Was she aware of my somewhat liberal view on the legalization of marijuana? That I despised hard rock music, and it made me feel anxious whenever it came on the radio? It was as if the floodgates had been opened and my imagined transgressions and confessions came pouring out. But did any of these things even matter in the scheme of our friendship? Mary was one of the least judgmental people I knew. It seemed I'd wasted a lot of years and written a lot of letters avoiding topics that I evidently could have discussed with ease.

So *what* possible topic could she feel apprehensive about broaching?

"Of course. You can ask me anything," I encouraged.

"You can tell me it is none of my business, if you want," she hedged.

I nodded. If Mary's reaction to my previous divulged secrets were any indication, she would not be fazed by my refusal to answer a question.

She visibly steeled herself, taking a deep breath before blurting out, "Do you ever miss sex?"

I laughed. There had been a few years in my marriage when I had been so bogged down by the mindless minutiae of mothering that I would have welcomed a lack of intimacy. But my post-cancer relationship with my husband had become more sexually charged. I did indeed miss sex, but not the act itself so much as that intimate physical connection with David, the man I loved.

"Yes, I sometimes miss it, but I think God is protecting me. That part of me feels as though it died when David died. I've even worried that if I ever met someone else, I would have to tell him I am broken." We both laughed at the choice of words.

"But, recently, I have felt stirrings of that part of myself, and I've also felt attraction to a man, so I realize I'm probably not broken. But if I ever meet someone, he is going to have to understand that I will still want to wait until marriage."

Mary nodded her head in understanding. She knew my faith and moral values. Would I have been able to tell just anyone these confidences? Not with the ease and sense of humor Mary and I shared.

I was glad for the topics this chapter brought up, as it convinced me there wasn't anything we couldn't discuss if we wanted to.

So who would you like to see as our next president, Mary? Because I think my vote's going to Ben Carson.

Mary Jedlicka Humston

"Enjoy your conversations with those around you today, ladies," the chairwoman announced at a Christian Women's Club luncheon years ago. "But we do ask you to refrain from talking about four things."

Having attended countless luncheons, I knew what was coming.

"Weight. Age. Politics. What church you attend."

We all laughed. Yes, weight and diet plans could easily monopolize a conversation until eyes glazed over. With age, it could be difficult to remain focused when hearing endless details of age-related aches, pains, and surgeries. But politics and what church you attend? Yes, those two could provoke some interesting, if not heated, discussions with anyone, anywhere.

Of those four, Mary and I have talked ad nauseam about weight and age. Some more about faith and church. But politics? Hardly at all. It's not that we're on opposite ends. In fact, I don't even know for certain what end she's on. It boils down to neither of us taking time to delve into that world to convince, change, or sway viewpoints.

I am uncomfortable talking at length with anyone about politics, so it's no surprise I wouldn't want to squander our valuable writing time. I vote. She votes. Or does she? Who we vote for and why is personal. Just to show how rarely we talk about it, I'll ask the question now. "Mary, what party do you support?" For the record, I'm an Independent.

Sex? Also personal. I never dreamed of sharing intimate details in letters to Mary. And neither did she, until . . . she was writing about her husband's cancer. I read the rough draft of her second book. Mary shared a tender scene where she initiated lovemaking for the first time after

David's cancer surgery and treatments. His reluctance stemmed from his perception about how he looked. Her gentle, loving words that he was beautiful touched the hearts of those of us readers who've had cancer, surgeries, procedures, or disfigurements that kept us from feeling beautiful, alluring, or sexy.

Still, even though I read that section, we never wrote to each other about it. The topic never surfaced again until we brainstormed chapter ideas for this book. Mary had suggested the chapter "Things We Never Write About." Sex made both our lists. It's an especially sensitive issue now that Mary is widowed, though we have briefly talked about that lack in her life when I tentatively initiated a conversation about it.

Money. Our early letters often reflected our mutual lack of having enough of it. We were one-income families. Finances were tight. We couponed and refunded. We shared economy-saving measures. It was only natural we commiserated in our letters.

Jim rose through the ranks at the fire department, attaining an officer position that provided more income which eased our financial life. We weren't rich, by any means, but we were able to contribute a certain sum for each child's college education, although they still had to work hard to save money, earn scholarships, and procure loans for the rest. On Mary's end, David had lost his job a time or two, and they went through hard times. We both understood each other's position, but we never pried. It boiled down to respecting privacy. I'm not saying we never wrote about money woes. We certainly did, but we tried not to dwell on them.

Family size was also a private issue. I had three children, while Mary's family continued to grow. Neither of us challenged the other for the decisions we'd made in that regard. She would no sooner ask why we stopped at three than I would question her having "yet another baby." We supported each other's decisions, realizing there are some issues that, even for us, are private.

Did this decision of family size impact our lives? Most assuredly. There was a time or two when I withheld some of my personal challenges from Mary so as not to overburden her. It was usually when she was pregnant, had just given birth, or was not getting enough sleep or "me" time to deal with her own problems, let alone mine. Now, with time and more frequent visits, I believe I've shared all those with her. And, as everyone knows, sometimes letters cannot do justice to a topic that is better shared in person. Writing about an incident requires more time than a face-to-face chat.

That doesn't mean deep feelings can't be shared. Oftentimes, the writing can produce benefits that in-person sharing can't: the starting and stopping, thinking, and trying to find the right words; the drinking of hot tea; the reflection. Sometimes it's easier to admit things in a letter than you can in person.

When I write Mary, it takes a couple of days for my letter to arrive—longer on weekends and holidays. Then, there's time for her to read and process it before she even sits down to reply back. Comments by this point are usually well thought out. Every word has been scrutinized to say just what it needs to say. While there are some topics we don't write about, there are countless more we might've had a hard time talking about. We let down our guard; we spill our guts and feelings; we adopt a no-holds-barred attitude. There is no censorship, and we write it as it is. Letters allow us to arrive at the meat of the issue rather than just nibbling at the the vegetables.

Drugs and rock and roll? For the record, Mary: yes, to early college drinking. But no, I've never indulged in illegal drugs. Not even marijuana. Not even an inhale. But rock and roll? I loved it as a teen, coed, and young mother. I usually listen to audiobooks in the car, but if I choose the radio instead, I'd likely go to Christian radio or rock-and-roll oldies stations. As for music at home? While I like a quiet house when I'm by myself, sometimes I'll put on music and do a little twirl or two in the kitchen. And I have special music for yoga.

But, yes, I rock 'n' rolled when I was younger. No apologies.

Soul Sister

Julia Theisen

Oprah Winfrey and I have one thing in common, and she said it best in her February 2015 column in *O Magazine*: "I am really good at working. Committed. Diligent. With stamina on steroids. Playing, I'm not so good at. I rarely decide to do anything just for fun."

I suspect, like me, Oprah was born serious. A worker. Too old too soon. At seven years old, while my friends were out playing, I would be indoors cleaning the kitchen on my own, because I wanted to! That more or less sums up my childhood, *taking on* responsibilities rather than *taking off* playing. This trait is a part of who I am and continues to manifest itself as I overdo things in many areas of my life. That is, unless I take time off to do something just for fun. Yes. I have now mastered how to do things that are inspiring and playful and simply for fun, with a little help from my friend.

Kari and I met when my husband and I opened our business. She worked with us as a representative from a local marketing company. Through working together, we discovered that we have a similar sense of humor as well as a similar heart and mind. We quickly became close friends. And then more than friends. We became soul sisters: "a woman friend who tends to the needs of our souls" (from *Soul Sisters* by Pythia

Peay). Kari was the female in my life that taught me how to do things *just for fun* and opened the doors of creativity within me. She expanded my soul.

The seed of that expansion started with a birthday gift. Kari suggested one year that we go to a nearby town for lunch. Wonderful. But, as part of that trip, she also invited me to make a piece of jewelry with her at a bead store. Not so wonderful. I truly believed that I had no idea how to create something like that. My mind took off as I envisioned Kari creating a designer-like, red carpet–worthy piece, while mine would resemble more of a cheap, amateur concoction. The idea of it made me nervous. Almost panicky. But sometimes that uneasy feeling in your gut can actually be excitement disguised as fear. And so, as Kari and I sat side by side, guided by the expert jewelry creator at the bead store, I surprised myself and created a beautiful necklace that I was genuinely proud of.

Looking back, I realize this first soul friend–inspired creative endeavor cracked open a door inside of me that had never before been opened. It turned my world from black and white to Technicolor. Since then, I've flung that door wide open, and have made lots of jewelry (I've dubbed my designs "Jules Jewels"), created personalized greeting cards, and written poems, among other things. I now see the subtle beauty and design that surround me wherever I go. Life and everything in it is my muse, providing inspiration for creative play time.

When I create, it fulfills a need in my soul. When I do things just for fun, I feel deeply satisfied. Every time I play, I know that I am healing my mind, body, and spirit. And it was my soul sister, Kari, who sparked that within me.

How do you repay someone for such a gift, the gift of your soul's expansion and deep healing? Well, with a soul sister, there's no need for repayment. There is, however, a wonderful opportunity to reciprocate, to feed her soul. And so it is that I have made Kari many cards, gifted her jewelry that I handcrafted, and composed this poem for a birthday gift:

Spirit of Generosity
Heart of a Healer
Sister to my Soul
This is You.
Beautiful. Inspiring. Sister. You.

The gift that Kari helped birth in me is now part of my way of being. These days I'm much more committed and diligent when it comes to play and having fun—just as much as I am with my work. So much so that this year, as I approached writing my New Year resolutions, I crafted them as "Soul Intentions," with the overall intention to be more. The word "be" means "to bring forth"—literally to bring forth more of ourselves. This was one of my Soul Intentions:

Playtime—*I'm aware that when I play more, I'm lighter and more receptive to the whisperings of Spirit. I do really well when: (1) I make beautiful birthday cards to gift to others, (2) I'm reading an inspiring book, (3) Scott (my husband) and I go to the movies at least once a month, and (4) I find a new play activity.*

Every woman needs a soul sister. A kindred spirit. One who is "loyal to the innermost essence, the deepest heart's desire, of their friends" (from *Soul Sisters*), who walks your journey with you to help you expand, and play, to do things just for fun, and to bring forth more of *you*. I am grateful that I have a soul sister that brings forth more of *me*.

With more than three decades of experience in the healing arts and twelve years of teaching yoga, Julia Theisen's passion is to help others be more fully themselves and live from a place of freedom in mind, body, and spirit. As founder of the Heart-Centered Yoga Teacher Training & Personal Transformation in Dubuque, she offers a variety of transformational workshops and programs. Julia is the founder and producer of the Dubuque Yoga Festival as well as cofounder and co-owner of three businesses dedicated to the wellness and healing of individuals and the community. See juliatheisen.com for more information.

CHAPTER TWELVE

Letter Writing 101

Dear Mary, how do you go about
writing a letter?

Mary Potter Kenyon

Who?

I'd grown up with a mother who obviously enjoyed writing and receiving letters. She rushed to check for mail each day, so it's no wonder a mailbox filled with treasures appealed to me. I was ten years old in 1969 when I spotted an offer for a free Super Ball on the back of a Cheerios box. An avid reader by then, I read anything in front of me, including the cereal boxes at the breakfast table. Soon I was receiving my own mail: refund offers I submitted with the labels from my mother's cabinets. To this day, I remember the thrill I received from the crisp dollar bills inside white envelopes addressed to me, or postcards with shiny silver quarters taped to them. Yes, that is how some refunds arrived in the '70s.

As a teen, I managed to entice a couple of my classmates to write real letters to me during summer break from school. With a demented sense of humor, my friend John sent used tea bags and fake mental institution commitment papers my way. Janice would write humorous letters using a name and persona that wasn't her own. These letters were addressed to a "Fred Potter." I'm surprised they were delivered.

I didn't obtain a real pen pal until I ran ads in magazines like *Women's Household* with pages of listings detailing photos, names, addresses, and interests. It seems quaint now, choosing potential pen friends by their common interests, but there were several magazines that included similar columns. As soon as they could print a few words, my children clamored to obtain their own pen pals through *Home Education* and *Countryside*. It was a sad day for our family when both magazines discontinued the practice due to the increase of weirdos who answered. We'd been contacted by a few. One man wrote to my son, asking him to conduct Internet research with a warning that he must never show the letters or the topics of research to his mother or sisters. A few declared their undying devotion to me, the mother they must have mistaken for single. Then there was the lonely widower who was looking to my teen daughter to care for his small children. He at least had the decency to call David to inquire into the appropriateness of moving to Iowa to be closer to Elizabeth. My husband let the grieving widower down easy, making it clear, however, that it was anything but okay.

We also discovered several gems among our ad respondents. A gentleman from England wrote Elizabeth for several years, and he even telephoned a few times. He sent books, cards, and beautifully written correspondence on fine stationery that our entire family passed around to read. Was he a rich eccentric, or a lonely old man? We would never know for sure, as he just stopped writing without explanation. To this day, some twenty years later, Elizabeth keeps in touch with pen pals from that era. She ended up marrying a young man she corresponded with for four years.

I had less luck in my attempts. Too often, my ads seemed to attract the more toxic sort: Debbie Downers who complained about everything, or worse, pathological liars whose stories didn't ring true. I even had one woman write about her disabilities and her husband's unemployment before asking if I could send her shoes and books for her children. We had our bookstore at the time, so I actually mailed a box shortly before my daughter got a similar letter, supposedly written by a girl her age whose parents had recently died. When the girl asked if Elizabeth had clothes or shoes she could share, we compared envelopes. While the stories and names differed, the handwriting was the same and so was the address. It was the odd request for shoes that had clued us in.

I also don't know what happened to the woman who'd suffered with chronic fatigue. I never heard from her again after she sent me dozens of medical journal citations and a twenty-page letter about the disease. I still have it in a file somewhere.

There are a couple of former classmates I've kept in touch with through annual Christmas cards and an occasional note. I also stay in contact with a fellow homeschooling writer who shares a passion for paper and the handwritten word, an elderly widow, and a few women I have met through writer's conferences in recent years. None of these snail-mail relationships come close to what Mary and I share. Mary is the first, and only, pen friend who has written with the intensity and frequency that my heart and soul must have yearned for in all previous failed attempts.

I also have a Tuesday ritual since my husband's death in 2012. David died on a Tuesday, and for a long time I dreaded that weekday, until I found a way to make it easier to bear, by reaching out to others through a card or a letter. There is no expectation of a response in these relationships.

What?

I've never really understood a need for a how-to book on letter writing, but when I consider the differences in my own children and their abilities, I realize it has been those who grew up writing letters who are most comfortable with it. Though I have always required each of my children to write thank-you notes, some of them have never corresponded beyond that.

As for myself, I never hesitate to write, not even when it comes to touchy subjects like an apology or sympathy card. I don't worry about proper formatting. I just write from the heart.

I've always been more comfortable expressing myself through the written word than over the phone. I'd rather write ten letters than make a single awkward phone call. As for email, it seems a poor substitute for snail mail.

When?

I pen most of my correspondence in the early hours of the morning. It's my preferred start to the day. I also like to write a letter to ease into work on a book or essay. Since my husband's death, I have also added Bible reading to my morning ritual, but the bulk of my pre-lunch hours includes writing of some sort. Ironically, with the intensity of work on this very book, my letters to Mary dropped dramatically. So did my Tuesday ritual of reaching out to others.

Where?

When I was the mother of very young children, my letter writing often came in snatched moments. Doctor and dentist waiting rooms could be counted on for beginning one on a notepad from my purse. For many years, I wrote Mary by the dim light of a nightlight in a child's bedroom. I never minded being asked to sit near a bed while one of my children went to sleep. Most of them learned to fall asleep to the soft sound of pen on paper.

Now, I usually sit on the couch, a cup of coffee (or tea if it is afternoon) nearby. When David was alive, I often wrote at breakfast while he sat companionably silent on the other side of the table, drinking coffee and reading the newspaper or a book.

How?

When Mary mentions our mutual love of paper and pens, I wonder if she knows the extent of my obsession. Would she be shocked at the contents of the cabinet where I store our school and office supplies? Three of the shelves hold paper; there are reams of white copy paper, stacks of colorful notebooks, bins of cute notepads, and brand new boxes of stationery. Then there is the seven-drawer plastic storage unit next to my desk. The bottom drawer holds scratch paper for grandchildren to scribble on, but the other six are crammed with vintage stationery, decorated printer sheets, and a wide assortment of note cards. I do have preferences: smaller stationery to the larger printer size, thinner sheets to the thicker ones, and vintage styles to newer ones. Thin air-mail sheets satisfy nearly all my senses. I feel a thrill of satisfaction when I fold the letter in half and hear the crinkling as I insert it in the envelope. Sometimes I take it out to re-read it just to feel and hear the paper again before mailing.

A scent of patchouli emanates from the incense sticks and soap bars I store inside the drawers of paper. I don't just like pretty designs—I want the paper to smell nice (like an old lady, according to my granddaughter).

While I love stickers, rubber stamps, and embellishments on envelopes, I don't take the time to use them. I'm fascinated by the concept of mail art. When I receive an elaborately decorated letter, I will look at it many times before I store it in a trunk where I keep favored correspondence.

My favorite pen changes, but I consistently have detested any fine-tip utensils or colored gel pens. I abhor erasable ink pens. I love the thick pens that are free promotional items from businesses. I wrote much of the first draft of this chapter using a fat ink pen with a comfort grip. "Iowa Prison Industries" is emblazoned on the side. When I find a writing utensil I like, I want more of the same, which is why ten packages of Bic Velocity black ink pens are in my cabinet. It didn't hurt that Bic distributed one-dollar coupons the same week Dollar General advertised a dollar sale on them.

Why?

Why do I write letters? Outside of the obvious fact that it's an ideal way to enjoy the paper I collect, I like the tangible way to connect with a fellow human being. And, of course, when I write a letter, there is always the hope that I will get one in return.

Mary Jedlicka Humston

Who?

Easy answer. Mary, of course.

I have loved writing and receiving letters since I was young enough to understand the joy of something *just for me* in the mailbox. I've had many serious letter exchanges in my life, especially during and after college and while Jim and I were engaged and lived hours apart. Then there was a lengthy writing relationship when my husband, daughter, and I moved to Iowa City in 1981 after living in Bellevue. Gloria and I spied each other across the room as we nursed our infants at a La Leche League meeting in the summer of 1980. When we moved away, she and I corresponded for a long stretch until she returned to full-time teaching. While we still write today, we don't have the frequency we had during those early mothering stages.

There's also Kathy M. from California who contacted me for more information after I had an article about playgroups published in the *Liguorian* in 1988. Once connected, we wrote copiously for a long time, and today we still write several lengthy letters yearly as well as exchanging seasonal cards. Our relationship deepened when we had the opportunity to finally meet in Palm Springs in 2013. My daughter Liz was attending a business conference there with her breastfeeding five-month-old, Zoey, and I had the good fortune to accompany them.

Then there's Kathy B., who recently moved to South Dakota. We met through a mothering magazine's pen pal section over twenty years ago. She should receive the "most patient" award when it takes me forever to reply back to her lovely, long letters.

But no other letter-writing relationship has had the frequency and longevity as Mary's and mine. We're in an entirely different category, and that's what makes this all so unique.

What?

What could we possibly have to say to each other, day after day after day? We pour our hearts out to each other, exposing every emotion imaginable. Mary is my sounding board. My second journal. My confessor. My way to relax. My daily muse. My daily news. Sometimes my letters are simply a blow-by-blow account of my activities. Sound boring? Not to us.

Naturally, our children have provided fodder. In the infant, toddler, and preschooler years, it was therapeutic to bemoan the lack of me time. Parenting issues and ideas on how to handle them traveled back and forth via the postal service. Teenagers. Sending them off to college. Their marriages. And now grandchildren. It's all been in our letters.

We also write about writing. Sharing the highs and lows of submissions, rejections, and acceptances were key elements as our productivity increased. We critique each other's work. In fact, chapters from this book arrived by mail for the other set of eyes to edit. We both know our suggestions will be viewed as a smorgasbord. Our editing motto has always been "Take what you want and leave the rest."

Our letters are never dull (maybe to others they could be, I suppose, but not to us). We're busy, active women with full lives, so I can't imagine a day when that nemesis, writer's block, will come between us. The list of topics will never dry up. It just won't happen.

When?

There is no ideal, perfect time when I write Mary. I have dashed off letters at all times of the day, though the wee hours of the night are sacrosanct. Working around active children in the beginning probably aided in my flexibility to write pretty much whenever I want.

Where?

I'm sitting in my queen chair in the front room. Chai tea by my side. Looking out the front window at the butterflies amid my phlox. The house is quiet. Ah, contentment.

Thus begins another letter to Mary. I'm not locked into that scenario (though I love my perfect-for-my-short-body chair that makes me feel like royalty). Take the car, for example. Motion sickness prevents writing while a passenger, but many letters to Mary were composed in a parked vehicle when waiting for school-aged children to finish piano lessons, religious-education classes, sports practices, or dance.

Notepads and pens nestled in my purse are at the ready for those snatched moments here and there when I can crank out a page or two. Or more. Writing while waiting proved a good use of time. A quick letter was better than no letter.

Late appointments provided another opportunity, depending on just how late "late" was. Countless letters sprung from the rooms of doctors, dentists, and hospitals, especially if I was alone.

I also love writing in my backyard. I'll bring out a pot of tea, covered with a dish towel to keep it warm since I don't own a tea cozy. I set it on a wooden bench next to extra stationery, pens, and Mary's latest letters. Bird and cicada songs, breezes rattling leaves, crisp air (especially in the fall), and sun reflections dancing in the yard provide the perfect backdrop. Once in a while, gnats, mosquitoes, and heat have intruded, driving me back in the house, but effective spray deters bugs most of the time. Accepting defeat and heading back to air conditioning seems to be the only answer to blistering heat. And Mary hears the details of my retreat.

When the kids were young and I could get away by myself for an hour or two, I'd often head to local fast-food restaurants in midmorning when the breakfast rush was over and order a large pop. I could sit in a booth, uninterrupted for a long time, and not only get a letter written to Mary but to other friends, too, all the while indulging in several free refills.

When vacationing or visiting our children and grandchildren for a few days, I try to send Mary a note. If not that, I at least send a postcard with a "wish you were here" as my postscript.

Anywhere there is paper, pen, and a good writing surface (propping up paper on a hard book or using a bunched-up blanket on my lap works well) can turn into a perfect place to whip off a letter.

In the late 1980s, I'd write sitting next to the bathtub while the kids splashed and played. Or I'd write outside at playgrounds. Letters weren't always smooth or coherent. Interruptions were constant. Trains of thought could be lost for minutes, hours, or even days before finding the unfinished letter somewhere in the house. These half-started scratchings buried under everyday detritus meant an extra bonus letter for Mary once it was found. Or, sadly, it meant a delay between the last one.

Neither of us is fond of no-mail days on Sundays or federal holidays. An empty mailbox is discouraging.

Recently, we attended a writer's conference with Veve, a mutual friend. In order to save money, the three of us stayed at Mary's brother, Lyle, and sister-in-law, Cindy's, home, less than a block from the main conference building. After one long but productive day, I unwound for the night in a cozy B&B-type bedroom and bathroom downstairs. As I brushed my teeth and washed off my makeup, I thought, *Hey, I still have time to write Mary.* I almost laughed out loud when it hit me. She was in the house, for heaven's sake. I only needed to climb the stairs and talk to her face to face. But my initial thought was *I can't wait to tell Mary all about what's happened today.*

How?

Mary and I are addicted to stationery. All kinds of it. We give it as birthday and Christmas gifts (usually in designs we fancy since we'll eventually be seeing those pages in our mailbox). We love free pens, pencils, and logoed pads from county fairs, businesses, motels, and hotels. Stickers adorn most of my envelopes. I'm also a fan of stamping designs on them.

If someone gives me a card with just my name on it and it isn't sealed, I recycle it, whiting out my last name and inserting Mary's instead. Cheesy? Maybe. Economical? Yes. Is there ever a time when I think I have too much writing material? I doubt it, though my husband might think otherwise.

My love for the *write stuff* stems, I'm sure, from my country-school days. I remember shopping trips in late summer to nearby Tipton, a larger town where we'd purchase supplies for the new year. Lined-paper tablets smelled luscious. Pencils stood as sentinels: crisp, smart-looking, and ready for action. Sharpening them provided another delicious scent. Then there was glue. Erasers. Rulers. Ballpoint pens as I got older. All of it excited me. Is it any wonder I grew up to be a paper, pen, and pencil aficionado?

I like gel writers or any pen that has a good grip. Having a multitude of free pens, it seems silly to purchase more. However, once in a while, I do. I can't help it.

Our letters are often messy, with no regard to correcting grammar, punctuation, or spelling. There is no logical organization. I can start one topic, skip to something else, and then circle back. Streams of thought create run-on sentences. Cross-outs, arrows, and ink blotches occur. If our letters had to be written perfectly or look pretty, we'd probably have abandoned this form of communication ages ago. We don't worry about length either. Some are short. Some read like novellas.

Through the years, I've used scraps of paper from my purse. Tiny notepads. Old envelopes. Fancy stationery. Goodwill purchases. Rejects from other people's stashes.

I remember one such stash. Years ago, Jo, a teaching colleague, had an assortment she no longer used and asked, "Would you want any of it, Mary?" Would I? While there was a good amount of beautiful stationery and cards, there were also some errant envelopes without matching paper and note cards with noncoordinating themes. I didn't care that it was a mishmash. It felt like a bonanza of bliss. I love anything I can use for writing. And I mean *anything*.

Why?

I've told Mary before that if a few (or heaven forbid, several) days pass and I haven't written her, I don't feel like myself. Who I am is so tied into our letter writing. I am a happier, healthier person when we regularly correspond. It probably keeps me sane and saves me countless hours and dollars of therapy, all the while offering another pair of listening ears alongside my husband's.

I write Mary because I enjoy it. It gives me peace. Pleasure. Purpose. Without our frequent communication, I'd be lost. It's that simple and that complex.

Postscript

Dear Mary, now that you've completed this
cowriting venture, do you have anything to add?

Mary Potter Kenyon

I f you'd asked me before I worked on this book with Mary, I would have said I knew most everything there was to know about her. The biggest surprise that came from our cowriting experience was the re- alization that, despite probably eight thousand letters between us, I didn't know her as well as I'd thought. There was an entire layer of friendship that hadn't been revealed through our letters. That layer was unearthed and scrutinized through months of working on this project.

In handwritten letters, we consciously choose how we will portray ourselves. Unlike face-to-face visits where body language and facial expressions might reveal unspoken thoughts, the letters Mary and I wrote revealed only what we were willing to disclose of ourselves and what each of us was capable of discerning through the written words of the other. That might explain why I didn't know the full depth of Mary's sense of humor or her faith until our visits were more frequent.

I didn't know the child, the teacher, or even the mother of one or two children that Mary had once been. Even though I thought I knew Mary, mother of three, writer, and active social butterfly, quite well, there was still so much that wasn't conveyed in thousands of letters. *You were home- coming queen, Mary? Why didn't I know that? There were things you didn't write about because you didn't want to add to my stress level? I thought you wrote about everything. I wasn't aware you'd held back sometimes.*

There was enlightenment, and then also relief. *You worried about that? You sound just like me!*

Mary and I have concluded that more visits would have added some- thing to our friendship, a depth that we've plumbed since that 2011 writ- er's conference when we spent a total of twelve hours in a car together and talked late into the nights at the hotel. I well remember tears during that lengthy visit, along with raucous laughter that had us doubled over, clutching our sides as we rushed to find a bathroom. Then there was more laughter as we imagined how we must look to others at the rest area off the highway.

Our friendship deepened even further after David's death in 2012, when Mary became the friend who took me out to eat once a month, holding my hand and asking those questions no one else dared to ask, then listening, *really listening*, to the answers. I learned about the "ship" part of the word friendship then, because without Mary, I'm not sure I could have kept sailing along.

As the deadline for this book approached, my brother, Lyle, and his wife, Cindy, graciously extended an offer of letting us use their empty house for a writing retreat while they were traveling. The first time we met there, Mary and I were practically giddy with the decadence of peace and quiet in a beautiful home with a sunroom view of a backyard filled with God's handiwork in plentiful plants, towering trees, and small animals that scampered in sunshine.

We put on a pot of tea, a necessity between these two writing friends. We could no more imagine writing without this hot sustenance than we could without pen and paper. We sat at the table to talk shop, sort through our notes, and make plans for the book. Then we settled down in the sunroom, giggling a little at the unexpected absurdity of our activity, editing within arm's reach of each other, like toddlers at parallel play.

It was a first for us, this shared writing time, but it was not the first time I'd sat and worked on a piece with another adult in the room. I'd shared that companionable silence with David for many years.

Mary pulled a pencil out of a case she carried, ready to slice and dice my work, circling things and writing comments on the side of the paper like she usually did. How many times had one of my essays come back to me in the mail with those same pencil markings? I suddenly wanted to use a pencil too, even though I've always used ink to mark up her pieces.

Mary chuckled a little when I asked if she had an extra pencil. For the first time in our relationship, we could actually view the process of mutual critiquing.

Later, while in the kitchen to refill our cups, I joked with Mary that I'd wanted to bring stationery with me in case I had time to write her. She reminded me of the previous summer when we'd stayed there. Downstairs getting ready for bed, she'd considered writing me a letter, though I was but a floor away. We wondered out loud why our letter-writing relationship had developed the way it had when other snail-mail relationships had not.

"There are people I write only once or twice a year," I marveled. "Why do you suppose we wrote so often? I think you must have been like a journal for me."

"I sometimes wish we had kept each other's letters," she mused. That comment made me wonder if it would have been just as difficult for me to read those old letters as it had been to read the journals and daybooks from my child-rearing era. While we wrote so often, it would have been the extreme highs and lows of my days that would have made it to the paper, not the day-to-day checks and balances.

That led me to ponder the "Oh, Baby" chapter I'd penned. I'd written it shortly after reading my daybooks in the fall of 2014. As a Christmas gift to myself that December, I'd had twenty Super 8 movies from 1984 to 1990 transferred onto DVDs. As I watched them, I remembered being a younger mother: one who decorated the table for childhood parties, who loved Christmas, who lay on the floor with a baby Michael propped up on her middle as she pretended to be asleep and then popped her head up to surprise him. Even in the silent movie, his reaction of a huge belly laugh was obvious. I thought about the husband behind the camera, the one who dearly loved the wife and the baby. I was reminded I had been a mother who was good at what she did. The smiles of those children in the movies attest to that. Watching them, I could remember being *that* mother. It wasn't all stress and strife, those years of parenting small children, as Mary had pointed out in her chapter. The journals gave an incomplete picture of what my life had been like then, just as our many letters had given Mary and me only part of the picture of the whole that was our lives.

And then there was the "Mothers" chapter. After reading Mary's interview with hers, I was jealous she still had a mom to interview. I could only conjecture and share my own impressions of my mother's past friendships. When I read the guest essay written by three generations of Neville women (after Chapter Two), I was reminded of the box I'd inherited, filled with my mother's letters she'd written to her mother. I also had her memory book. For an entire afternoon, I "visited" with Mom through these. Her memories of childhood friends were happy ones. She'd enjoyed their company and fun times. When she changed schools, she'd been welcomed warmly. Though she indeed encountered her own mean girls, the brief mention hints that she was not bullied mercilessly like many of her own children had been. A "Beverly" is mentioned many times, and from a letter Mom had written to her mother, I discovered both a maiden and a married name. "Perhaps I'll be able to visit Beverly in Cedar Rapids," Mom had written. The fact that she knew where she lived suggests they kept in touch. Sure enough, with the maiden name to guide, I found Beverly in Mom's address book. Did my mother ever get that chance to visit? To reconnect with an old friend? Thanks to the Internet, I unearthed an obituary. Beverly outlived her eighth-grade buddy by four years.

As for friends while she raised children, the letters dated 1961 through 1979 explain a lot. Gardens, canning, plucking chickens, washing loads and loads of laundry, making homemade rugs, curtains, dolls, and dresses. There was simply no money and no time for friends.

The one question I would have asked my mother—"Did you ever experience a lifelong friendship like mine and Mary's?"—was answered thusly: "I always had my invisible friend, my Guardian Angel."

That answer was both comforting to me—she always felt a spiritual guide—and poignant—there was no lifelong friendship mentioned, though I knew she'd considered my father her best friend.

Mary and I came up against many obstacles in the course of writing this book. In fact, in the months between signing a contract and turning in a completed manuscript, there were times when we turned to each other in complete dismay. Because we'd felt God's blessing on this project all along, we were determined to forge on, despite what came our way. What came my way during a period of five months were health challenges in the form of suspicious mammogram results, a concern with my blood sugar level, and a knee that began aching shortly after I'd signed the book contract, culminating in pain so bad I had trouble sleeping by the manuscript's end. My son Michael experienced a house fire, and his dog lived with us for a few weeks while repairs were done. My assistant at the library began having health problems around the same time Mary and I began our cowriting venture. Midway into the manuscript, I faced the loss of many free writing hours when I took over my assistant's workload. Then there were the car troubles. The weekend I planned to visit my brother's house for a lone writing retreat, my vehicle practically blew up on the side of the road. While I gave up on the retreat idea, I had to borrow my daughter's car the next day to get to a speaking engagement. The brakes went out on the way there.

I saw the extent of Mary's determination as she faced her own demons—most notably, bouts with vertigo. I got to see another side of her that hadn't been fully revealed though our letters: her stubbornness.

"Mary is a lot more like me than I realized," I told my daughter Elizabeth on the phone.

"Maybe if Jim dies someday, you and Mary could live together," was her reply.

Without thinking, I'd blurted out in horror, "Oh, no, she'd drive me crazy!"

Mary laughed when I confessed this transgression one day at my brother's house.

"We're too much alike," she agreed.

"Can you even imagine not writing each other?" I asked then.

I saw tears well up in her eyes.

Later on the way home, I let myself briefly consider a life without Mary's letters. I couldn't bear it.

I thought again of what my daughter had suggested, that Mary and I live together someday, and this time I could picture it. Aren't there things about anyone we might live with that annoy or irritate us? Didn't I have to adjust to living with another human being when I married David?

I love Mary. She is one of the first people I turn to in both good and bad times. Cowriting this book with her has drawn us even closer. Yes, I can imagine us living together as two old (much older!) widows. Would we want to continue writing each other even though we lived in the same house?

That would work. I own more than enough stationery already for the both of us.

Mary Jedlicka Humston

Once our proposal was accepted—on, of all days, Halloween—*Mary & Me* became our number one priority over pretty much everything, except our families and her job as the Winthrop Library director. I've enjoyed cowriting with Mary, and I know she'd say the same, since the process has produced some interesting experiences.

After Mary's initial announcement at a speaking engagement that her next project would be working with me on a book about our letter-writing friendship, we naturally discussed this idea in our letters. The reality took root during brainstorming sessions in the community room at the Manchester Public Library. We'd eat at a local tearoom, check out her sister's consignment store, and then head to the library. There in that private, comfy room, we hatched the premise of *Mary & Me* and thought of possible chapters and marketing ideas.

Two activities remained constant for me along the way. One: drinking hot tea. I consumed so many cups that the stash in my cupboard diminished to where it needs restocking. Yippee! Tea shopping here I come! The other? Using Marsha's blessing prayer. Saying it while working on this book gave me comfort and direction.

The majority of my chapters were created with pencil and scrap paper before being typed into the computer. There was just something about my fingers holding the pencil and my arm and hand moving across the paper that provided satisfaction difficult to derive from computer composition. After that, Mary and I read, over and over, our rough drafts, our tentative final copies, and the finished chapters going into our main file. Even after ferocious editing and scrutiny, we missed glaring errors, which was why we appreciated each other's continuous critiques.

Mary repeatedly heard my declaration: "All good friends should cow-rite a book. Their friendship will deepen beyond measure." We laughed, of course, because we knew few would do this, but our resulting discussions created an even stronger, more durable relationship.

Working on the book consumed copious amounts of time, so much that I frequently joked with my other friends, "I'll be lucky to have any friends left after I write this book on friendship." Again, there was laughter from these dear ones who pledged, "We'll all be here when you're done." Hallelujah.

Not long after penning the short paragraph about the traffic accident on my family's way to church, I received a surprise in the mail. My cousin Nancy sent me correspondence between her mom and our Grandma Loretta culled from her recently deceased mother's boxes of memorabilia. In one of her letters, Grandma told Aunt Sue about the accident. What are the odds that Nancy would find letters detailing that event, from all those years' worth of correspondence, and then take the time to mail them to me? I immediately called her and shared the coincidence. Or was it?

Iowa City hosts the Iowa River as one of its most prominent community members. It runs through town and timber with occasional trails constructed along its banks. When we moved here in 1981, I don't recall spotting eagles anywhere. Since then, an explosion of the avian freedom symbol has occurred. Rarely can I walk or drive along the river during winter without spying these magnificent birds. One day, with less than two weeks before the manuscript deadline, the pressure got to me. I decided to take a walk along the Iowa River trail, hoping to spot some eagles to inspire me. The highest number I'd counted on my walks so far this winter had been eighteen. I don't factor in the ones flying—only those perched. When I pulled my car into the parking lot at Napoleon Park, I had already discovered a dozen in the trees across the river. Before my one-hour walk ended, I stopped counting when I'd reached one hundred. Talk about inspiration.

I had several odd dreams during the early months when the ratio between finished and unfinished chapters favored the latter. While the dreams were all different, they contained the same theme. I was running around trying to accomplish a task only to find roadblock after roadblock. I stood behind our church altar in one of them, where it was imperative I read prayers as a stand-in for the priest. Naturally, the book of prayers was missing. Helpless, I faced a waiting congregation, trying to rely on memory. When it didn't come to my rescue, I remained, humiliated, until being whisked away to a different inexplicable setting.

In another dream, I was a speaker at a large event. A scene of running warren-like hallways and desperately asking how to find the room kept looping over and over with different people and places but always with the same result: I could never find it. When I finally located where I was to speak, I didn't have my speech. Aghast, I bolted through the congested halls again out to the parking lot, but this time I was unable to locate my car where my precious notes resided.

As more chapters of the book were completed and edited, these odd dreams mercifully ended.

When we talked about meeting at Lyle and Cindy's for several Saturdays, we both assumed our workday would find us relaxing in comfy chairs out in their sunporch, composing chapter after chapter. That didn't happen. Instead, we handled business details, critiques, editing, and decisions on guest essayists, promotional blurbs, and potential speaking engagements. We laughed. We cried. We drank tons of tea, but we didn't sit in companionable silence and create new chapters.

Challenges dogged us along the way. Iowa blizzards and snowstorms frequently canceled our work plans at Lyle and Cindy's home. Since we both had long drives, we knew it wasn't worth the risk of trying to out-maneuver winter's fury. Outpatient surgery removed skin cancer from near my eye and required recuperation time. I missed a step in a dark restaurant and fell hard, injuring my left rotator cuff and requiring weeks of physical therapy and exercises. Vertigo and light-headedness plagued me around the holidays. I'll stop there lest anyone suspects I'm making this all up.

One of the more mysterious surprises was my inability to read books. I typically finish one to two per week, sitting in my queen chair in the evenings. For some reason, this rarely happened. I easily finished magazines and daily newspapers. A few inspirational books were read, but they took days to complete. One Christmas novel hooked me with the usual fervor, as did two youth novels about the Underground Railroad, and I listened to several audiobooks, but the rest of the time, there was a dearth of reading. Puzzled, I can only wonder if my mind was inundated with words for *Mary & Me*.

I shouldn't have been surprised in the final weeks before submitting our manuscript that our letter volume decreased significantly, but I was. Instead, emails reigned, probably more in those weeks than in the entirety of our correspondence period. I look forward to returning to what has linked us all these years: those good old letters.

Mention must be made about my husband Jim's contributions. It became obvious when I'd forget to eat while working on the book that intervention was needed. During the final weeks, he planned menus, grocery shopped, and prepared healthy meals. Colorful bouquets brightened the computer work area as well.

Exciting events also occurred during this time. Jim and I celebrated the joy of Levi Jon's arrival in late November, our son and his wife's first child. Two grandchildren turned two years old, and our oldest grandson will become a five-year-old soon. There were five holidays during this time: Halloween, Thanksgiving, Christmas, New Year's Day, and, of course, the unofficial fifth one, Super Bowl Sunday.

What a journey it's been to cowrite with Mary. I anticipate even more highways and byways to explore. Happy traveling to us, Mary. Happy traveling.

Suggested Resources

Books about Friendship

Friends for the Journey by Madeleine L'Engle and Luci Shaw

The Friendship Crisis: Finding, Making, and Keeping Friends When You're Not a Kid Anymore by Marla Paul

Friendship for Grown-Ups: What I Missed and Learned Along the Way by Lisa Whelchel

Heart to Heart: Deepening Friendships between Women at Midlife by Patricia Gottlieb Shapiro

I Know Just What You Mean: The Power of Friendship in Women's Lives by Ellen Goodman and Patricia O'Brien

A Prayerbook for Spiritual Friends by Madeleine L'Engle and Luci Shaw

Books about Letter Writing

Always First Class: The Pleasure of Personal Letters by Lois Barry

Gift of a Letter by Alexandra Stoddard

Good Mail Day: A Primer for Making Eye-Popping Postal Art by Jennie Hinchcliff and Carolee Gilligan Wheeler

The Hidden Art of Homemaking by Edith Schaeffer

If You Find This Letter: My Journey to Find Purpose Through Hundreds of Letters to Strangers by Hannah Brencher

The Letter Writing Project by Wendy Wolff

Signed, Sealed, Delivered: Celebrating the Joys of Letter Writing by Nina Sankovitch

Snail Mail My Email: Handwritten Letters in a Digital World by Ivan Cash

To the Letter: A Celebration of the Lost Art of Letter Writing by Simon Garfield

Writing Personal Notes & Letters by the editors of *Victoria* magazine

Blogs and Websites for Letter Writers

The Great Letter Revival

tglr.blogspot.com/

This is a movement to bring back genuine, personal, creative, and meaningful human connections to our modern world via letter writing. Join their Facebook Page, www.facebook.com/TheGreatLetterRevival.

365 Letters

365lettersblog.blogspot.com/

This letter-writing project began in 2009. Carla Mckeown blogs about many different letter-related topics, including stamps, letters in the news, stationery, and more.

Everyday Should Be a Red Letter Day

redletterdayzine.wordpress.com/

This blog, written by Jennie Hinchcliff, an artist and instructor in San Francisco, focuses on mail art and related topics.

The Letter Exchange

www.letter-exchange.com/

Published three times a year, LEX is a great way to find pen friends through listing your own pen pal ad, or answering others'. Whether you want to discuss contemporary events, brag about your cat, connect with other crafters, or compare opinions on the latest bestseller, this newsletter is a great way to find pen friends.

Letter Writers Alliance

16sparrows.typepad.com/letterwritersalliance/

Established in 2007 by Kathy Zadronzny and Donovan Beeson Yothers, the Letter Writers Alliance is dedicated to preserving the art form of the handwritten letter. Become a member at letterwriters.org.

The Missive Maven

www.missivemaven.com/

This letter-writing blog extols the virtues of "snail mail" and all its accessories.

A Penchant for Paper

http://apenchantforpaper.blogspot.com/

Heather has been blogging since 2008 on all things paper. Fellow addicts can join her blog.

Pencil Revolution

www.pencilrevolution.com

An entire blog based on pencils? You bet. Based in Baltimore City, *Pencil Revolution* is brought to you by blogger Johnny Gamber, who enjoys writing and editing things.

SocialJane

www.socialjane.com

Social networking site SocialJane is dedicated to providing women with a quick and convenient means to meet and connect with other like-minded women as friends with interests that match your own.

Viva Snail Mail

www.vivasnailmail.com/

Melissa Lohman-Wild sends out handmade mail regularly, hosts *MAKE MAIL* workshops for children and adults, and posts weekly on her blog. Melissa holds an MA in media studies from The New School. She lives in Brooklyn, New York, with her husband and two mail-indoctrinated kids.

WriteaLetter.org

writealetter.org/main/

WriteaLetter.org is an international nonprofit educational forum dedicated to encouraging and preserving the art of the handwritten letter
and a haven for all things related to the handwritten letter—stationery,
cards, pens, ink, inspirational books, pen pals, support, and all sorts of
encouragement.

Pertinent Articles for Further Study

Berkovitz, Gail. "UCLA Study on Friendship Among Women: An
Alternative to Fight or Flight." 2002. www.anapsid.org/cnd/gender/
tendfend.html

Hall, Alena. "9 Reasons Not to Abandon the Art of the Handwritten Letter."
The Huffington Post, January 11, 2015. www.huffingtonpost.com/
2015/01/11/benefits-of-writing-letters-and-postcards_n_6425540.
html

Rubin, Gretchen. "Five Secrets of Lifelong Friends." *Good Housekeeping
Magazine*, August 2011. www.goodhousekeeping.com/health/wellness/
advice/a18150/five-secrets-to-lifelong-friends/

Williamson, Martha. "Signed, Sealed, and Delivered." *Guideposts*, June 2014.
www.guideposts.org/positive-living/overcoming-negativity/doubt/
signed-sealed-and-delivered

Discussion Questions

Chapter 1: First Meetings

The thing about real life is that important events don't announce themselves. Trumpets don't blow, drums don't beat to let you know you are going to meet the most important person you've ever met, or read the most important thing you are ever going to read, or have the most important conversation you are ever going to have, or spend the most important week you are ever going to spend. Usually something that is going to change your whole life is a memory before you can stop and be impressed about it. You don't usually have a chance to get excited about that sort of thing . . . ahead of time.

—Edith Schaeffer

1. Meeting Mary H. was a momentous occasion for Mary K.—finally, the kindred spirit she'd yearned for. For Mary H., the encounter was just another in a series of first meetings. When you meet a prospective friend, which of the Marys are you most like?

2. Mary K. put strict requirements on who she would accept as a friend, essentially limiting potential friendships. Have you ever done this?

3. Do you think Mary K. would have even liked the "clone" she desired if she'd ever discovered her? If such a thing were possible, would you like yours?

4. Can you remember a time when a casual introduction turned into a deep friendship?

5. Letter writing deepened the authors' friendship after Mary K.'s move. Have you had a friend move? If so, what happened to your friendship? Discuss activities or events that might deepen a long-distance friendship.

6. Neighbors. Coworkers. Organization and club members. These situational friendships sometimes don't last once the situation has changed. Has this happened to you? Or did the situational friendship remain?

Chapter 2: Mothers

But there's a story behind everything. How a picture got on a wall. How a scar got on your face. Sometimes the stories are simple, and sometimes they are hard and heartbreaking. But behind all your stories is always your mother's story, because hers is where yours begin.

—Mitch Albom, *For One More Day*

1. Mary K.'s mother had not been an example in regards to adult female friendships. How important do you think it is to be a role model to your daughters in this aspect?

2. Both Mary K. and her mother struggled to balance a tight budget with raising babies. Do you think it is harder for a mother who is struggling to make ends meet to develop friendships? Why or why not?

3. Mary K.'s mother was afraid to tell her friend about her cancer, worrying that she would tell her "I told you so" about her smoking. Are

there any friends you would hesitate to share a cancer diagnosis with?

4. Mary H. enjoyed interviewing her mom about her friendships. What questions would you ask your mom about friendship? What other questions might you like to ask her?

5. Mary H. had never heard about Nancy, her mom's friend who had tragically died in a fire. Have you ever learned anything about or from your mother that surprised you?

6. What do you remember about your mother's friends?

Chapter 3: Mean Girls

I am still every age that I have been. Because I was once a child, I am always a child. Because I was once a searching adolescent, given to moods and ecstasies, these are still part of me, and always will be.

—Madeleine L'Engle, *A Circle of Quiet*

1. Meeting a former classmate's sister at a hair appointment thrust Mary K. back in time. Have you ever had something similar happen when meeting someone from your past?

2. Do you think the clothes children wear can make them a target for bullies?

3. Mary K. believed a single friend made a difference in how she was treated when she entered junior high. Have you had a similar experience?

4. Has a single comment like "Gee, you're fat" eaten at you? Has something someone said recently hurt your feelings?

5. How did you make friends when you were younger? Did your friend-making skills change as you grew older?

6. What qualities do you value in a friend today?

Chapter 4: Oh, Baby!

The natural state of motherhood is unselfishness. When you become a mother, you are no longer the center of your own universe. You relinquish that position to your children.

—Jessica Lange

1. Are you familiar with attachment-style parenting? What does that term mean to you?

2. Do you have sisters? If so, do you consider them friends, as the authors do? Do you think women need friends outside of their own families, or can sisters or sisters-in-law be enough?

3. Do you agree that isolation can contribute to a sense of paranoia? Have you ever felt isolated?

4. What stressors did (or do) you experience as a mother of young children? What were (or are) your coping methods?

5. Did you latch onto a support group like Mary H. did with her playgroup? Explain why you did or didn't need it.

6. What can mothers with young children do to carve out time for themselves?

Chapter 5: The Write Stuff

It's a fallacy that writers have to shut themselves up in their ivory towers to write. I have all these interruptions, three of which I gave birth to. If I was thrown for a loop every time I was distracted I could never get anything done.

—Jodi Picoult

1. Do you find yourself saying you "don't have time" for an activity you'd like to pursue? Mary K. found time for writing, even while

raising eight children. Does her experience encourage you or discourage you from pursuing your own passion?

2.   Mary K.'s husband didn't support her writing in the early years, though he redeemed himself later on. Why might a spouse fail to encourage the hobby or interest of their partner?

3.   Mary K. considered her mother a muse of sorts, and her husband the "wind beneath her wings." Do you have people in your life that have influenced your pursuits?

4.   Writing was one way the Marys' friendship was cemented. What activities solidify your friendships?

5.   Writing for publication is a rollercoaster of emotions. If you're a writer (or know one well), explain why this is true or not true.

6.   Both friends find journaling important in their life. Do you?

Chapter 6: In Sickness and in Health

Armed with my positive attitude and inherent stubborn nature, I keep my mind focused and my life moving forward. I stop to rest, pout, and even cry sometimes, but always, I get back up. Life is giving me this challenge and I will plow through it, out of breath with my heart racing if I have to.

—Amy B. Scher

1.   Both authors experienced a "mystery illness" within months of each other, at a time when there was little known about immune system disorders. Do you have a friend or a family member that suffers with chronic fatigue syndrome, fibromyalgia, or a related condition? After reading this chapter, did you gain a little more understanding of what they might deal with on a day-to-day basis?

2.   Both Marys had a difficult time getting a diagnosis for their illness. Have you ever experienced the frustration of seeking medical help

and not finding answers? Do you know someone who has?

3. It's difficult enough to be chronically ill, but having young children when experiencing illness adds another dimension. How do you think having a chronically ill mother affects a child?

4. Have health issues ever affected one of your friendships? If so, in what ways? How did you and your friend handle the medical issues? Or didn't you? Have you ever had a friendship end because of illness?

5. Neither author mentions support groups, although Mary H. attended one meeting after having thyroid cancer. Have you ever sought a support group? If so, did it help you?

6. How can you help an ill friend? Brainstorm and try to put into practice one of these ideas for someone you know who is dealing with an illness.

Chapter 7: When Jealousy Rears Its Ugly Head

You can only be jealous of someone who has something you think you ought to have yourself.

—Margaret Atwood, *The Handmaiden's Tale*

1. Mary K. rationalizes that all relationships inevitably include some envy. Do you agree?

2. What do you think Mary K. means when she states that "the face of envy is not becoming on anyone."?

3. Do you agree that jealousy is an uncomfortable emotion?

4. Has jealousy ever threatened one of your friendships? How did you handle it?

5. What are the types of things that make you jealous of your friends?

6. Can jealousy between friends ever be a good thing?

Chapter 8: Who, Me? Worry?

Worry does not empty tomorrow of its sorrow. It empties today of its strength.

—Corrie Ten Boom

1. Have you ever experienced the "monkey mind" that Mary K. describes? Did her description help you understand anxiety?

2. What do you think about taking medication for anxiety?

3. Do you think a propensity for anxiety can be inherited, or is it more of a situational factor?

4. Both authors deal with anxiety and try to help each other with its challenges. How can you help a friend dealing with anxiety?

5. What makes you anxious? If you have anxiety issues, have you ever shared that with a friend? Why or why not?

6. Healing from anxiety can't be measured like healing from a broken bone can. How does this challenge a person with anxiety?

Chapter 9: Losses

The English language has about 450,000 commonly used words, but more may be needed. What do you call someone who has lost a sibling or had a miscarriage? Or a gay person whose partner has died? Or an elderly person who has lost every friend and relative? So many heartaches can't be found in the dictionary.

—Jeffrey Zaslow, in *The Wall Street Journal*

1. Have you experienced the loss of a friend through death? Or through other circumstances? How did you handle that loss?

2. Would you describe your spouse as your best friend?

3. Have you hesitated befriending someone older than you?

4. What are some of the deepest losses you've experienced? How did you get through the hardest times?

5. Mary H. helped Mary K. through the concurrent losses of her mother, husband, and grandson. How can you help others get through loss?

6. Do you think there is a difference between a sudden death and one that causes lingering suffering and pain? How can you help a friend in either situation?

Chapter 10: Faith

Faith is taking the first step even when you don't see the whole staircase.

—Martin Luther King Jr.

1. Mary K.'s original idea of what constituted a person of faith seems closed minded, and more about church doctrine and rules than Bible edicts. Do you know people like this?

2. Mary K. didn't think she could be a good Christian unless she followed her mother's faith walk. Why do you think that is?

3. Have you experienced some type of turning point in your own journey of faith?

4. Are your friends mostly from the same faith or belief system that you hold?

5. Do you feel comfortable sharing your faith when you don't know where someone stands in that area?

6. Has faith ever been a divisive issue in a friendship? If so, how did you handle it?

Chapter 11: Sex, Drugs, and Rock & Roll: What We Don't Talk About

I hadn't realized how much I'd been needing to meet someone I might be able to say everything to.

—Elizabeth Berg

1. The authors hadn't talked much about politics in three decades of letter writing. Do you talk politics with your friends?

2. Mary K. hesitated to discuss her worries about educational choices her family had made with Mary H. Why do you think she feared judgment on that issue?

3. The two friends never broached the subject of sex until after one friend lost her husband. Is this a topic you avoid discussing with your friends? Do you know someone who overshares in that area?

4. What topics have you refrained from sharing with friends?

5. How important is confidentiality when discussing sensitive issues? Have you ever had a friend betray your confidences? How did it make you feel? How did that affect your friendship?

6. What are some topics you would never share with a friend? Are you surprised by some of the topics never discussed by the two Marys?

Chapter 12: Letter Writing 101

I don't want the words to be naked the way they are in faxes or on the computer. I want them to be covered by an envelope that you have to rip open in order to get at. I want there to be waiting time—a pause between the writing and the reading. I want us to be careful about what we say to each other. I want the miles between us to be real and long. This will be our law—that we write our dailiness and our suffering very, very carefully.

—Siri Hustvedt, *What I Loved*

1. Mary K. seems to have strong feelings about what kind of paper or pens she prefers. Do you share this foible, or understand it?

2. Does Mary K.'s penchant for stationery seem perfectly rational, or does there seem to be a problem bordering on hoarding going on?

3. If you are a writer (of letters or otherwise), do you have a favorite spot for the craft?

4. When you write letters, what utensils and equipment do you prefer to use? Why?

5. Do you find letter writing a chore? Or a joy?

6. In this age of social media, how do you feel about snail mail?

PS: Postscript

To me, reading through old letters and journals is like treasure hunting. Somewhere in those faded, handwritten lines there is a story that has been packed away in a dusty old box for years.

—Sara Sheridan

1. Mary K. discovered many things about her friend through the process of writing a book together. Were you surprised at how much she didn't know about Mary H., considering those eight thousand letters that passed between them?

2. Both Mary K.'s maternal grandmother and her own daughter Elizabeth met their prospective spouses through the mail. Do you think you can get to know people well through the mail, or, for that matter, through dates, when obviously they might only show the best of themselves either way?

3. Is there a friend close to you that you could imagine living with someday?

4. In a perfect world where all things are possible, which friend would you like to cowrite a book with?

5. What are some questions you could ask your dear friend that might enhance your friendship?

6. What was the most important takeaway lesson you received by reading this book?

About the Authors

MARY POTTER KENYON graduated from the University of Northern Iowa with a BA in psychology. She is the director of the Winthrop Public Library and is widely published in magazines, newspapers, and anthologies. Mary is a popular speaker and workshop presenter at churches, writing workshops, women's groups, and grief support groups. Check out her website at www.marypotterkenyon.com for information about her public speaking repertoire and scheduled events. This is her fourth book with Familius. She is the author of *Coupon Crazy: The Science, the Savings, and the Stories Behind America's Extreme Obsession* (August 2013), *Chemo-Therapist: How Cancer Cured a Marriage* (April 2014), and *Refined By Fire: A Journey of Grief and Grace* (October 2014). Mary lives in Manchester, Iowa, with three of her eight children. You can write her "real letters" at 816 East Butler St., Manchester, IA 52057 or email her at marypotterkenyon@gmail.com.

MARY JEDLICKA HUMSTON, a former high school teacher, graduated from the University of Northern Iowa with a BA in English education. She has had over 150 poems and essays published at the local and national level in newspapers, magazines, books, and online. One of her poems was chosen to be projected on the Krakow UNESCO City of Literature *Poems on the Wall* in 2014. Mary has presented programs on cancer, dealing with chronic illness, prayer, writing, and the Little Free Library movement. She is a member of the National League of American Pen Women and the University Club Writers of Iowa City. Mary lives in Iowa City with her husband, Jim. You can write her "real letters" at 1425 Franklin St., Iowa City, IA 52240 or email her at maryjedhum@gmail.com.

The authors maintain a blog on letter writing and friendship at www.maryandmebook.wordpress.com and a Facebook page at www.facebook.com/MaryandMebook.

About Familius

Welcome to a place where parents are celebrated, not compared. Where heart is at the center of our families, and family is at the center of our homes. Where boo-boos are still kissed, cake beaters are still licked, and mistakes are still okay. Welcome to a place where books— and family—are beautiful. Familius: a book publisher dedicated to helping families be happy.

Visit Our Website: www.familius.com

Our website is a different kind of place. Get inspired, read articles, discover books, watch videos, connect with our family experts, download books and apps and audiobooks, and along the way, discover how values and happy family life go together.

Join Our Family

There are lots of ways to connect with us! Subscribe to our newsletters at www.familius.com to receive uplifting daily inspiration, essays from our Pater Familius, a free ebook every month, and the first word on special discounts and Familius news.

Become an Expert

Familius authors and other established writers interested in helping families be happy are invited to join our family and contribute online content. If you have something important to say on the family, join our expert community by applying at:

www.familius.com/apply-to-become-a-familius-expert

Get Bulk Discounts

If you feel a few friends and family might benefit from what you've read, let us know and we'll be happy to provide you with quantity discounts. Simply email us at specialorders@familius.com.

Website: www.familius.com

Facebook: www.facebook.com/paterfamilius

Twitter: @familiustalk, @paterfamilius1

Pinterest: www.pinterest.com/familius

The most important work

you ever do will be within

the walls of your own home.

CPSIA information can be obtained
at www.ICGtesting.com
Printed in the USA
FSOW01n1413210416
19530FS